SO YOU ARE GOING CONTRACTING

Freelance YOUR way to Freedom

2nd Edition

PAUL REYNOLDS

Copyright © Black Chili Limited 2021. All rights reserved.
First paperback edition printed in 2015 in the United Kingdom
Second paperback edition printed in 2021 in the United Kingdom

A catalogue record for this book is available from the British Library.
ISBN: 978-1-911064-13-8

No part of this work may be reproduced or transmitted in any form or by any means, electronic or mechanical, including photocopying, recording or by any information storage and retrieval system, without the prior written permission of the publisher.

Published by Black Chili Limited
For more information, please email publications@blackchili.co.uk

Every reasonable care has been taken in the creation of this publication. The publisher and author cannot accept any responsibility for any loss or damage resulting from the use of materials, information and recommendations found in the text of this publication, or from any errors or omissions that may be found in this publication or that may occur at a future date, except as expressly provided in law.

Masculine pronouns such as 'He' and 'His' are used throughout this publication for consistency, but no gender bias is intended.

SO, YOU'RE GOING CONTRACTING – 2nd Edition

INTRODUCTION 1
ABOUT THE AUTHOR 5
ARE YOU READY FOR CONTRACTING? 9
THE CONTRACTOR TALENT MATRIX 11
   QUALIFICATIONS 13
   SKILLS 15
   EXPERIENCE 17
ISN'T CONTRACTING RISKY? 21
MAKING THE TRANSITION 25
YOUR CV 29
FINDING YOUR FIRST CONTRACT 33
   THE ADVERT 33
   THE APPLICATION 35
   THE INTERVIEW 37
   THE OFFER 41
   STARTING THE CONTRACT 45
GETTING PAID 47
   PSC / UMBRELLA COMPANIES 49
   SOLE TRADER / PARTNERSHIPS 53
   LIMITED COMPANY 57
SETTING UP A LIMITED COMPANY 61
   REGISTERING WITH COMPANIES HOUSE 61
   OPENING A COMPANY BANK ACCOUNT 65

VAT Registration 67
Filing a VAT Return 71
Insurance **73**
Professional Indemnity 73
Public Liability Insurance 74
Employers' Liability Insurance 74
IR35 Insurance 74
Running a Limited Company **77**
Security 79
Get a Good Accountant 83
Company Website 85
Register a Domain Name 87
Hosting 89
The Site 89
Email 91
Bookkeeping **93**
Invoice Summary 95
Invoices 99
Expenses 103
Bank Statements **107**
Storing Documents 108
Company Stationery **109**
Letters 111
Business Cards 113
Email Signatures 113
Tax **115**
VAT 117
Corporation Tax 117

PAYE	118
LIMITED COMPANY PAYROLL	119
PAYROLL DEADLINES	120
TAX CODES	121
TAXABLE BENEFITS	121
SELF-ASSESSMENT	122
COMPANIES HOUSE ANNUAL RETURN	123
NATIONAL INSURANCE	**125**
PENSIONS	**127**
IR35	**129**
WHAT IS IT?	129
INSIDE OR OUTSIDE?	131
THE KEY CRITERIA	133
WHAT IF I'M INSIDE IR35?	135
IR35 COMPLIANCE	136
IR35 ENQUIRIES	137
IR35 RECOMMENDATIONS	139
MAXIMISING YOUR INCOME	**141**
TAKING HOLIDAY	143
THE CONTRACT MARKET	**144**
TRAINING	**147**
IR35 DEVELOPMENTS	149
SO YOU'VE GOING PERMIE	151
THE RESOURCE SITE	**155**
SO YOU'RE GOING CONTRACTING TOO!	**157**
CONTACTING THE AUTHOR	**159**

Introduction

So, getting on for five years since 'So You're Going Contracting' launched to widespread critical acclaim! Well, made it to #1 in the enormously popular 'business books – consultancy' chart on Amazon where I suspect there isn't much competition. Regardless of that, I guess that makes me a best-selling author!

I wrote the first edition of this book in response to friends, colleagues and professional acquaintances thinking contracting was difficult, time consuming, inherently risky and basically beyond them. And it isn't. Many of the books available on the subject are absolutely massive. I'm sure that makes them more comprehensive and full of very useful information, but I am also sure that you don't need all that information to get started – so if you want only the information you need to get going as a contractor, this book is for you!

However, much has changed in the years since the first edition, and an update is probably long overdue… so here it is! There will be similarities with the previous edition, as well as new material, most notably in light of the ever-changing and somewhat opaque legislation and regulatory framework that surround it. What was a passing mention of 'IR35' in the first edition is likely to become a lengthier affair this time around. Hopefully it'll be clearer and more concise that the source material!

So you're going contracting too? Or at least having a think about the pros and cons of it. Great plan! And one that has served me well for many years. Enabling more professional progress and working freedom, as well as a lifestyle few salaried jobs would enable. Where the permie bunch refer to contracting as 'the dark side', those of us already here know you're about to see the light. Congratulations on finding the courage to look around and consider your options.

The road that leads people to contracting is often long and winding. Maybe you're feeling jaded by the working world, working long hours whilst not reaping the rewards you feel you deserve.

Perhaps you crave the freedom of being self-employed, the self-determining satisfaction that will come from building something yourself and enjoying the benefits of your success instead of watching somebody else doing it.

This book now represents over fifteen years of experience in contracting. It imagines the 'day one' scenario that you've made the decision to go contracting, takes you through finding work before progressing to options for payment vehicles, company setup and everything you will need to do to be ready and running as a contractor. Life for a contractor has certainly gotten more complicated in the years between the first edition and today but if I can do it, so can you.

In the following pages you will find real world hints and tips, and examples of all the key documents you'll need. There are, of course, considerable resources available to you with books dedicated to each of the subject areas in their own right, but this book gives you everything you **need** to know to get contracting in a complete but concise package. Contracting may appear daunting, but it is actually very accessible – and doesn't take nearly as much work as you might imagine. Once you have read this book, you'll be in a position to start on the road to contracting, and once you are on your way, this book will remain a helpful reference throughout your new career.

About the Author

I left University with an English Literature degree and like most people with English degrees who have no inclination to go into teaching; I had no idea what I was going to do. I fell into a resourcing job for a recruitment company... calling people and talking to them on the phone about technology jobs I didn't understand, and getting paid minimum wage. I have that terrible job to thank for setting my future direction.

My last day at that company started uneventfully enough, until one of the many people I called that day unwittingly showed me the light. He was pretty horrible actually – I'd called him regarding a contract that was obviously some way beneath him. He was direct, to put it mildly – and his parting words were, 'So you can update your records, I wouldn't take a permanent role for less than £250K'. **Two hundred and fifty thousand pounds?** (and this was in 1999!) At the rate I was going that would be 25 years' wages. And that was my light bulb moment.

It can't be that hard, I thought. To quote Sir Nicolas Winton, **'If it's not impossible, there must be a way to do it'.** And thus, my journey began. I looked at the skills required for some of the serious consultancy roles, I was spending my days trying to fill, then researched what the jobs that fed those sorts of positions were. Having followed my nose to the entry level of the field, I set about acquiring the skills required to get through the door. I worked my way through the ranks in several jobs, which at the time I didn't much appreciate, all of which allowed me to build solid experience with some of the biggest companies in the world.

I studied for professional qualifications on my own time, self-funding courses and exams – investing in myself. I took my last permanent job with one of the 'top five' consultancies having been sold what I thought was a great job at a great company. Perhaps I'd set my expectations way too high before I got there, and it couldn't fail to disappoint; and sure enough I wasn't satisfied. When I got a call offering me my first contract I was very interested, but I was going to have to get from 'Eh?' to 'Done' very quickly to make it happen.

Set up a company, get a bank account, find an accountant, register for VAT, get some professional insurances, deal with agents, go for interviews, get a contract, review the contract, get the contract checked, sort the invoicing, learn basic book keeping, develop the discipline to keep decent records... and we've not even started the day job yet! These elements, and so many more, need setting up and sorting out to enable self-employment. From a standing start the task can seem herculean, but the approach is the same as when eating an elephant – one bite at a time!

I have been working as a freelance consultant for over 15 years, and prior to making the transition I had no experience at all of either establishing or running a business. I have since become a director of several companies and feel comfortable with all aspects of business. I started in the same place as you... with a big learning curve in front of me. By sharing my experiences, I hope to make that curve less daunting for you.

Are you ready for contracting?

Feeling ready for contracting is a largely personal thing – you're ready when you decide you're ready. There are many factors to consider, and if you've been cocooned in the world of salaried permanent employment, it may be that habit that proves the hardest to break. The existential question of whether you are ready in terms of mental preparation is important, though less directly related to your future financial success as a contractor than your skillset. This section deals with the more pragmatic elements: have you got what it takes to be a successful contractor in professional terms?

This boils down to qualifications, skills and experience.

The easiest way to judge whether you are ready for contracting is to take a look at the advertisements for available contract roles and measure yourself against the bar being set, just as I did. If your skills, qualifications and experience meet the requirements of a contract you would like to be offered – then yes, you are ready for contracting. You might even want to consider reaching up for the next rung of the ladder!

But what if they don't?

If your CV does not fit well with the kinds of contracts you aspire to, a GAP analysis can be undertaken quickly and easily to establish what you need to rectify the situation. Make an honest assessment of where you are, and consider how to get from there to where you want to be.

Guidance for addressing any shortfall follows.

The Contractor Talent Matrix

The modern contractor requires a broad, adaptable and evolving set of talents to thrive in a competitive marketplace. The ratio of components differs across sectors, but they are all vital to succeeding as a contractor.

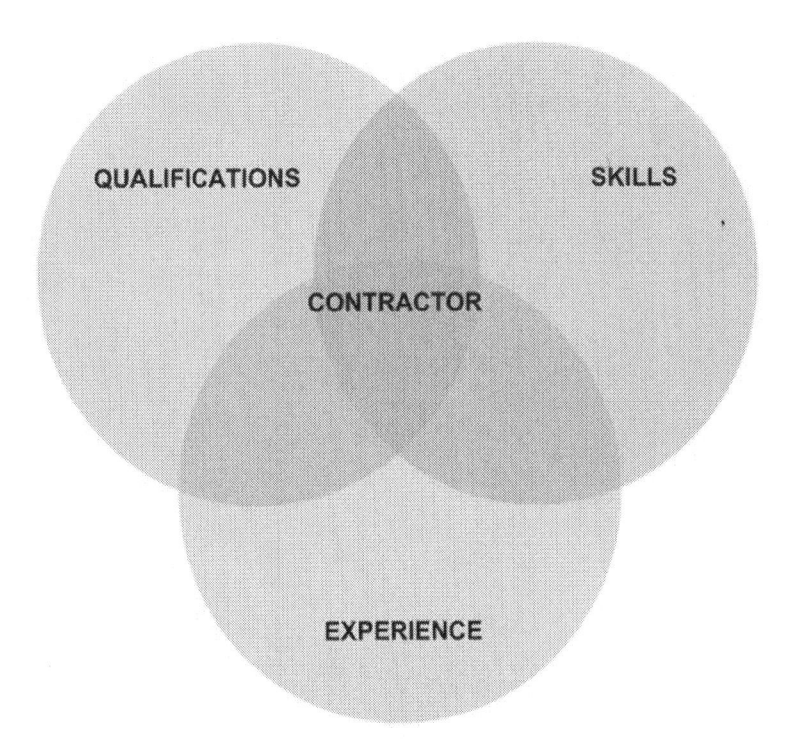

QUALIFICATIONS   SKILLS

CONTRACTOR

EXPERIENCE

As a contractor, you are expected to be on top of your chosen game, able to hit the ground running without anyone needing to 'show you the ropes'. Your client is paying you and your company for a service, and it is vital for your success that you can provide that service competently and professionally.

Qualifications, skills, and experience are all critically important to contractor success:

- Acquire them to build competence and confidence.
- Communicate them on paper to agents to be put forward for contracts.
- Communicate them to clients to win the contract and get work.
- Demonstrate them to earn contract renewals, repeat business and referrals.

Contractor life is much, much easier with all the right boxes checked. The following pages will help you if you are not there already.

Qualifications

If a contract requires a specific qualification without exception, look at similar roles and see if they, too, demand the same qualification. If the qualification has become a common prerequisite of a particular job and you want that contract, you may have no alternative but to seek that qualification. Prince2 for Project Management, TOGAF or Zachman for Enterprise Architecture, ITIL for service management, Cloud certifications for engineering – all these have become standard, and client expectation will be that all the applicants will have them. It follows therefore, that all agents will look for them, and you may find yourself out of the running pretty fast without suitable qualifications.

The good news is that training is available and can be surprisingly cost effective. Residential courses are available that will give you the training and the certification (assuming you pass the exam) in shorter timescales than traditional training. It is, however, important to possess the skills as well as the certificate - so I would only advocate a crash course to formalise the skills and knowledge you already largely possess.

It is equally possible to study on your own time thanks to the Internet. A huge number of training providers have popped up in recent years, with training materials and exam prep information available at various price points.

Investing in yourself is both wise and worthwhile, and keeping up to date with training and qualifications remains important once you are contracting. More often than not, it is those not in possession of the right sets of qualifications who perceive them as being unimportant or irrelevant.

If you are in permanent employment, it may be possible to secure training via your current employer, which will benefit you in the future as well as your employer today.

Employers may, in some cases, ask you to sign a contract on receipt of training compelling you to reimburse them the cost of said training should you leave their employment within a specified amount of time... in which case, carefully consider the pros and cons before you proceed.

I experienced the opposite situation; a company I was working for offered me a significant training programme, but I had already decided I wanted to move on. I told them I could not accept the training, as I didn't feel my future was with them. It was a difficult conversation to have, but a necessary one.

You can't put a price on integrity, and once you are contracting your reputation will become the very essence of your business. Without it, you will very quickly have nothing.

Skills

If a contract requires very specific skills, they may be a non-negotiable requirement for the advertised role. Still, the first step is as discussed in the previous section - to review listings for similar roles and establish whether the requirement for a specific skill is commonplace or even ubiquitous. Assuming the skill you are missing is one you require; you have two options.

You could acquire the skill. Practically, that means learning it and applying it in your current place of work. It may be possible to teach yourself a skill on your own time. Perhaps a friend or colleague could help you acquire it. You will need to apply your freshly acquired skills in a way you can demonstrate or convey to a client, or at least feel confident enough that if called upon, you could respond with a calm and reassuring confidence.

Ultimately, if the skill in question is a requirement for all contracts of a particular type, you will absolutely need that skill – or spend an awful lot of time anxiously trying to avoid it. It is only a matter of time before that becomes a problem. And problems like that will eventually have a negative impact on your contribution to client work, ultimately with reputational consequences.

Your second option would be to bridge the gap between your most relevant skill and that being requested. For instance, if you lack the skills required to create a spreadsheet using LibreOffice, but you have got the skills to create one using the Microsoft or OpenOffice equivalents – it is likely that the skills you have are close enough to those required that the journey from one to the other is achievable. The similarities are sufficient for a client to accept your skills with another product as adequate. Suggesting your top score on Pacman stands you in good stead for creating a spreadsheet might be a tougher sell, but if you can create a persuasive narrative... you never know.

Ultimately in this set of circumstances the client gets to decide whether he believes the distance between your most relevant experience and his requirement is acceptable, and you get to judge whether you'll go grey or bald running between two points that are further away than you're letting on.

My recommendation for both success and sanity is to acquire any necessary skills and be confident in them before offering them effectively as services. The alternative is risky to reputation and livelihood, as well as setting you off on a path of possibly perpetual anxiety.

Unless you are adept with smoke and mirrors of course – I have known several management consultants like that!

Experience

Contracts will often request experience of specific tasks - management of so many direct reports, budgets of so many millions, rollouts, migrations, specific technologies, upgrades, projects of particular types, public sector, banking, number of years served... you name it.

None of these are standard, so should you find yourself falling short of the mark for a particular role, option number one is to find an alternate contract with a much-reduced experience requirement. Problem solved! This time anyway. The longer-term options for a prospective contractor lacking experience are similar to those for acquiring the absent skills outlined above.

You need five years of project management experience to be a contract project manager? The best bet, therefore, could well be to work as a project manager in permanent employment. Start in a more junior role if necessary and get to your five years' experience before embarking on contracting with the entrance requirements satisfied. Yes, that would work. If it were that simple, you would then be a contract project manager for the rest of your working days, with those five years' experience gradually building. It is sensible and necessary to possess solid skills and experience before setting out as a contractor, but those skills and experiences grow as we progress, and it is communicating that progress that is key here.

Draw upon relevant experience, perhaps a history of embracing and overcoming new challenges throughout your career. You may have previously managed so many projects simultaneously that you could be a portfolio manager. Add that to the time you spent being an escalation point for other managers, and providing some oversight - and you're a programme management candidate. Maybe you've been an engineer for so long that you're now a design authority. It is important to recognise your own professional progress, regardless of whether your current job title adequately reflects it.

Most contractors have progressed through the ranks in a similar way to their permanently employed counterparts and have done so without the need for direct experience to move to the next level. Relevant experience is almost as good and having a demonstrable drive to succeed is a quality any client will appreciate and respect.

You might also consider volunteering as a means to build experience. Charities, small companies and local companies as well as schools, societies and clubs often have a need for some of the talents common in the corporate world for their boards and internal governance structures, as well as needs to specialist help from time to time. You could take advantage of an opportunity to gain some experience and return the favour by donating your time and talents to those who would benefit from them. Everybody wins.

Qualifications are easy to prove, and skills are relatively easy to acquire with a time commitment and dedication. Experience is perhaps the most difficult element to communicate yet the most highly prized. All the qualifications in the world are no substitute for real-world experience, and it is ultimately that experience that a client is paying a premium for a contractor to get.

Isn't contracting risky?

Ah… one of my favourite questions, and the comment I most often hear from permanent employees.

Maybe I want to be impoverished? Perhaps I don't care about my wife and children? Failing that I must surely be insane to accept the lack of security that comes with contracting.

Perhaps these individuals lack the self-belief and fortitude to go contracting themselves and are seeking to justify their on-going plough of the same furrow. Anybody not working in a steady permanent job must be nuts, right? I mean, whoever heard of a company going under or staff being made redundant in their thousands with seemingly no notice? Never happens doe it…

Now, I'm not suggesting for a moment that contracting is without risk. But then neither is being in conventional employment. And you are, in my view, far less likely to fire yourself if times get hard than someone else would be to fire you in the same circumstances. Ask yourself what you actually stand to lose in swapping the warm and snuggly permie cocoon for contracting:

- Security and stability in permanent work? Questionable, and prone to change.

- Training and development, courtesy of your employer? Questionable, and prone to change.
- Holiday allowance and Sick Pay? – Fine, I'll give you that one. Contractors don't get those.

However, the latter is more than adequately compensated for by a drastic income improvement. Keep in mind as well that all an employer is doing is keeping back some of your salary to pay you while you're not working, they're not doing their employees a favour by just gifting them money, no matter how much we might like to believe that!

And aren't all the risk factors better off in your hands than someone else's anyway? Yes, yes they are!

Employees often perceive themselves as being more secure than they really are. The reality is that if you are confident in your own ability, and have the skills and experience the market demands, you would be consistently employed as a contractor. In over 15 years of contracting, I have only been out of work either for periods in which I did not wish to work (such as the six months I took off work when my son was born), or a week or two between contracts, which was also planned and I will explain the rationale for in the coming pages.

If you are the kind of person who 'coasts' in a job – doing the bare minimum to get by, taking no interest in career development or progression, taking no responsibility for your outcomes and are generally content to spend your entire working life (let's not forget this accounts for more of your time than anything else) staying pretty much where you have always been... contracting might not be for you. If you're keeping your head down for pension day or a redundancy payment then again, contracting might not be for you either.

If you're good at what you do, skilled and experienced at least adequately for your current job and those you immediately aspire to, and willing to take ultimate responsibility for your professional destiny you will be at least as successful as a contractor as you have been as an employee.

In short, **if you are good at what you do, there is no risk associated with contracting**.

Making the transition

Making the transition from permanent work to contracting need not be any more complicated than finding that elusive first contract. If you've arrived at a point that you are considering a change of job, why not consider contracting as well as permanent opportunities? This flexible approach also applies to contractors – many of whom may opt to take a permanent role, seeing it as another contract – albeit potentially longer term. Consider everything on its merits.

Contract roles are often advertised as being 'urgent' with applications encouraged immediately and interviews in a matter of days. This can seem daunting to traditional employees, who are used to a more relaxed and even ponderous pace. The reality in my experience is somewhat different, and clients looking for contract resources can be just as selective with the individuals they choose as those looking for salaried staff; everyone wants the job done right after all.

Make sure you leave your current employment gracefully. Serve the notice term stipulated in your contract of employment and be straightforward with everyone. Your current employer will expect it but will still be appreciative and will hopefully give you a solid reference if you conduct yourself professionally. Your prospective employer will respect your integrity and fortitude in following through on your commitments. As an employer, I might be frustrated to have to wait for someone to start working for me, but I wouldn't be very impressed to hear they had skipped out on their notice leaving their employer in the lurch. If they've done that to one employer, presumably, they'd willingly do the same to me if a better option presented itself.

My main piece of advice here is the same, regardless of the employment status of the job you're looking to leave or the one you're hoping to start. Never burn a bridge. Even if those on the other side of it have given you every reason to. Maybe they have conducted themselves such that you'd never go back there if they were the last employer on earth. You will discover – if you have not already – that it really is a small world, and there is every chance that you will run into old colleagues, bosses and direct reports in your professional future.

Even if you have satisfied yourself that the bridge in question is of no value at all, tread carefully. If the company you're working for today is going bust tomorrow, your boss will also be looking for a job. And karma having the cruel sense of humour it so often seems to, you can pretty much bet the person you screw over today will be the one in the hiring manager's chair tomorrow.

And it would be pretty awkward if the intern whose life you made a misery for years ended up being the hiring manager for your next contract, wouldn't it? Whether we care to admit it or not and whether we like it or not, relationships are famously important... it's not *what* you know... you know.

Make sure you use your notice period to establish and build your network. Connect with people you've worked with and for via the various social channels, exchange email addresses and make sure to keep in touch. Contacts are a valuable resource and making the effort to cultivate and nourish relationships will pay you back one-hundred-fold.

Your CV

It is imperative you have a solid curriculum vitae (CV) for success in securing work regardless of the contractor or permie debate. Also known as a 'resume', no doubt you already have one, and it has served you well enough to secure the job you are in. It will, however, almost certainly benefit from an update.

Key information to present in a CV includes:

- Personal details including name, contact number(s), email address and any professional social media profile. A date of birth is no longer required, owing to age discrimination rules, and full address has also fallen out of fashion, replaced by city or town.
- A short but strong statement of who you are professionally and what your aspirations are is helpful for a permanent job, less so for contracts. However, hiring managers often expect to see it so please include it. Such things help provide context and tell a client a bit about who you are. You need to fit in with their team.
- Job history should include the following for each role; position, start and finish month/year, name and location of employer or client and a summary of achievements, tasks, duties, projects and major programmes of work undertaken. Focus on the achievements

though – you want prospective clients to see what hiring you gives their organisation.
- List academic qualifications and achievements in order of importance. Provide full detail for your highest-level academic qualification and progressively less as you continue. For example, you might give your university degree classification, main area of study and any interesting notes before listing A-levels as only subject and grade, and GCSEs as the total number achieved at a passing grade unless any are of direct relevance to the role in question. If document length becomes an issue, consider dropping all but the highest qualification unless directly relevant to the role.
- List professional qualifications and courses in full, and using the same approach as above – the highest and/or most relevant qualification first. Again, consider dropping the least impressive on the grounds of space, should the need arise.
- Finally, a 'personal' section where you can list other things about you – interests, hobbies and other points not suitable for inclusion elsewhere. It is an inexact science, but people naturally like people who they believe to be similar to themselves. Let the reader know who you are and what you're about.

It is recommended that you chose a standard font for your CV in the Arial, Verdana or similar family – clear and easy to read. Embolden and underline for emphasis as necessary. I have personally had great success adding graphics to my CV to draw attention – logos for professional qualifications in my case, which add a bit of colour and interest.

General wisdom is that a CV should not exceed two pages in length, but that can get difficult for a contractor – I have been contracting for over fifteen years and my CV became six pages long. It didn't cause me any obvious issues and I never received negative feedback, but I trimmed it down to three pages by starting with the most recent, interesting and impressive elements of work history and become increasingly brief in summary while working back, Should the reader tire of my CV before the end, he will have absorbed the most salient points before he stops reading. For the same reason, academic and personal information comes at the end.

As an exercise, it can be interesting to try to fit your whole CV on a single page, ensuring the message is strong and no space is wasted. You can then use the lessons learned to communicate your professional life more succinctly. Achievements above everything else!

I am also aware that experts recommend tailoring your CV to a specific role, but I do not believe this works as well for contractors. Remember that you are operating as a company providing services; as such the service you provide does not change based on the client requirement.

It is possible, however, that your CV does not show a skill or experience you possess which is listed as essential in the contract advertisement, and in those circumstances it is recommended you include it. Usually CVs are submitted electronically, and you may fall foul of the selection process at an early stage if your CV is not returned in an agency search against relevant key words.

Machines these days perform the first pass, so do make sure any relevant keywords appear in the text. Otherwise, your CV may not even get in front of a real life human!

It goes without saying that a good CV should be checked for spelling and appropriate use of punctuation. If in doubt, ask a friend or trusted colleague to review it for you.

A CV template can be found on the resource site:

https://www.blackchili.co.uk/bcbooks

Finding your first Contract

Finding contract work is, in many ways, similar to finding a salaried job. You would look for adverts in newspapers, trade publications and specialist websites, such as www.jobserve.com or www.indeed.com and get the inside track from friends, colleagues and those in the know.

The main difference is that instead of working with the company that has the requirement (known as 'the client' in contractor terms) you would typically deal with an intermediary, or agency. The agency will broker all dealings with the client during the process of securing the contract, and in many cases throughout the contract as well. With the exception of the interview, it is very unlikely you will speak to the client directly until you have started the contract.

Flash forward to slightly less certain times, and direct engagements with clients are more common than they once were thanks to new regulatory frameworks, but the road in remains similar.

The Advert

So – you find a contract that looks good to you. You need to consider:

- The rate: there are (typically) 7.5 hours in a day, 37.5 hours in a week, and 48 weeks in a year (allowing 4 for holidays). Use this information to calculate the

various remuneration permutations and compare them to your current package.
- Status: IR35 rules make the take-home pay of an 'inside' or 'outside' contract very different. A good rule of thumb being that the contractor would need 30% more 'inside IR35' to match earnings 'outside IR35'. More on this later.
- The location: the cost of commuting, as well as time commuting. Will you need to stay away from home overnight? All these expenses can be offset against tax when outside IR35, but it still means money leaving your pocket.
- Contract duration: things change, and notice periods are there for a reason on both sides, but a six-month contract with likely extension listed is probably a better bet than a two-week contract for a specific task. Obviously depending on your own circumstances.
- The fit: is the contract a good fit for your skillset? You are only as good as your last contract, so you need to be confident you can deliver against the listed requirements. Getting the job is one thing, doing it and doing it well are something else entirely.

The Application

You've read the ad, and thought about the points above. You're going to apply – so what do you need to know?

- A solid Curriculum Vitae (CV) is a must. If you have a friend or colleague who has made the transition to contracting, ask to see theirs. Refer to the CV section for real world tips that have served me well over the years.
- When you apply, make sure to take time over the email or application form; nothing turns off a reader like poor grammar or spelling. Particularly when most word-processing applications check such things for you at the click of a button.
- Follow up with a phone call. Agents typically work with a specific client requirement and do the first round of applicant filtering themselves. They may, for instance, be sending 10 CVs over to the client with six applicants being called for interview. That means once the agent has sent across 10 CVs they consider suitable, yours will not be forwarded, even if you're better qualified. Call the agent under the guise of checking if they have received your CV, using the opportunity to build a relationship and improve your chances.
- Request updates. Agents typically get more applications than they have slots for interviews - never mind available

roles. Keeping in touch with the agent communicates a determination to progress, and if you are not selected you have an opportunity to gather feedback that will help your next application.

The agency will make all the necessary arrangements, and assuming you are selected for an interview, all the details will be sent to you – usually via email.

The same process applies to client-direct engagements, but be extra mindful that your persistence in dealing with the HR department, if over-zealous, could be detrimental to your contract seeking efforts. The route between them and the hiring manager is much more direct, and consequently all communications have less of a filter.

The Interview

I've had all kinds of interviews over the years, from a 'technical interview' where I was asked whether I knew Windows, and then asked when I could start (!) to a multi-stage panel interview with an assessment centre day. These are both extremes, with your likely scenario landing somewhere in the middle.

Typically with contracting, a phone interview will be the first stage. Depending on client requirements and your performance it may, in fact, be the only stage. Following a successful outcome, a face-to-face interview is likely; probably with the hiring manager or a senior team member.

The skills that have stood you in good stead in your working life thus far continue to apply: be punctual, courteous, and dressed appropriately for the contract in question. You will notice an absence of some of the vacuous questions asked in standard interviews:

"What does a 'Bob Jones' bring to our organisation?"
'Where do you see yourself in five years?'
'What makes you interested in a career with ACME Co.?'

Fortunately, for contract positions, all these questions and many like them are totally irrelevant and not typically used. You are applying for a specific role, usually for a precise and limited duration. All questions, therefore, will be geared toward establishing your suitability for the task at hand. Nothing beats direct experience in this stage of the game. If you can demonstrate that you have executed the same duties previously, any company will take notice of that.

If you have not had direct experience of the required tasks, do everything you can to establish links between your most relevant experiences and the role. Honesty and integrity are paramount for contractors but bridging a modest divide between your skillset and a contract is perfectly acceptable. For example, perhaps you haven't worked with the word processing or database package that the client favours, but you have used several others and have a solid grasp of the underlying concepts. Turn that potential perceived weakness into a strength by communicating a solid foundation of skills, and a capability to acquire new skills quickly – key qualities for any contractor.

Confidence is very important; personally, I have found it almost as important as experience. I was offered a very senior role with a 'top five' consultancy company simply by saying 'I'm confident I can add some value there' in response to every question. And I'm not kidding. I didn't take the contract, because frankly their approach bordered on insanity, but was offered it purely on the confident and capable impression I gave. You don't want to come across as arrogant; aim for a calm and easy manner, which imparts a sense of a capable and confident professional who is comfortable with the task at hand.

Once the interview has concluded, give the agency a call where applicable to let them know how you feel it went. Be honest, the agent may not know the client well, and all these interactions help build relationships that may be helpful in the future.

A suggestion based on experience – never sound too excited about a particular role. This may prove beneficial to you when negotiating assuming you are offered the contract; you want to stay in a strong position to do so.

The Offer

So, you're about to be offered your first contract? Exciting times!

The client or their agent will contact you to inform you of the offer and the details – notably the rate, duration and the start date. They will also want to know how they can pay you in due course, and you'll find out all about that in the next chapter.

It may be that a rate has not until this point been specified or discussed; perhaps you have been given an indication of the budget the client has at his disposal.

It is at this point a contractor and his client or agent may find themselves with opposing interests. The contractor of course wants to maximise his income. The client would like to spend as little as possible and the agent would like you to work for as little as possible; many agents will then absorb the rest of the contract rate as profit. Lovely for them, less good for you. There are judgement calls to be made from all sides:

The client: Could pay a little more to get you to take the contract. Doing so would get them the contractor they have selected and would save them the time, effort and expense of re-advertising the contract as well as another interview cycle.

The agent: Could pay you a little more to get you to take the contract, making less profit in the process. Doing so will satisfy client direction and make them money, the agent is unlikely to make more by re-advertising a role and finding someone else to take it for less money. And it is a lot of work for them

The contractor: Could probably take a slightly lower rate to get the contract quickly and easily but may then be on that lower rate for any subsequent extensions.

Having taken into account any travel, accommodation and subsistence expenses have a figure in mind you will not drop below. The client or their agent will absolutely have a figure they cannot go above... and your task is to get as close to that line as you possibly can. Having been chosen by the client you are immediately in a strong position, and some gentle enquiry around increasing the rate should be very achievable.

If your agent is on a fixed percentage, it will be in their interests to maximise your income so as to maximise theirs. That doesn't necessarily mean there is no room for negotiation. If your skills are niche, or you know you're a strong candidate for the role it is possible to convince the agent to give you some of their commission back. Not common, but it happens.

Final thought. I once finished a contract and had planned to take a couple of weeks off before finding the next. I got a call on the drive home on my last day for a new contract to start immediately, which was paying 15% less than I had been hoping to achieve. I turned it down and took a contract two weeks later as I had planned. Only much later did it occur to me that it would take me some six months of work at the rate I had achieved to recover the two weeks earnings I lost by not taking that lower paying contract two weeks earlier – although I did enjoy the break.

Sometimes, a bird in the hand really is worth two in the bush.

Starting the Contract

Your first day in a contract will be very similar to your first day in any job: figuring out the logistics, meeting the team and finding your way in a new environment. Typically, there will be no sedate introduction to the new office; the client is after all paying a premium for your services. It is very likely that after pleasantries have been exchanged you will have been provided with some documents to review to help set the scene, and will be expected to pick up and run pretty quickly.

Don't panic - rely on your skills and experience. Confidence can again be your friend, and don't be afraid to admit when you don't know but undertake to find out. Good consultants will routinely find themselves on the fringes of or completely outside their comfort zones, constantly having to evolve and acquire new skills. There is no shame in not knowing, provided you have the capability and resourcefulness to find out in short order.

From the beginning, relationship building is crucial. The people around you may have a very immediate say on your contracting future, and they will almost certainly have one in 3, 6 or 12 months when renewal time approaches. Being capable is expected but being personable is a less common trait. And one that will serve you well.

Getting Paid

Being a contractor means selling your services to the client or their chosen agency as a company rather than directly as an individual. It is very important to distinguish between a company as an entity, and yourself as the consultant of that company.

You have three main options:

- A Personal Service Company (PSC), often known as an 'Umbrella' company as it typically covers many freelance workers.

- A sole trader / non-formal company

- A limited company

Many contractors will opt for the umbrella company route in the first instance as it offers a quick and simple path to market. If you are offered a contract today with a start date in the next 14 days some sort of managed service is worth considering.

For 'inside IR35' engagements, you may find yourself obliged to use an umbrella company, perhaps one on a list of preferred suppliers. In this case, there is no option aside from not taking the contract.

Longer term and for those serious about contracting outside IR35, my recommendation would be to take the limited company route.

Many clients and most agencies will not deal with sole trader structured companies, and PSCs can be expensive. PSCs are also not as appealing on close inspection as they may have first appeared. Let's explore why.

PSC / Umbrella Companies

There are several umbrella companies available, and their offerings are broadly similar. The basic idea is that you work under their company banner – they receive payments from the client, and then pay you via standard PAYE. They will also process your national insurance contributions.

Typically, setting up as an umbrella contractor can be done in a day or two. The umbrella company will give you a 'take home' figure based on your contract rate, and you as a contractor will likely be required to complete weekly timesheets. The umbrella company will then raise invoices on your behalf and process all payments. The administrative fee they charge you will cover a specified number of holiday and sick days, normally available after a qualifying period.

You can also choose to have all those deductions passed to you as you earn. This is highly recommended a some less-scrupulous umbrella companies will absorb any retained holiday pay in the event of holiday not being taken!

Sounds good? The main downside of using an umbrella company is the scale of the fees, which can mean a 20% reduction in take home pay compared to running your own limited company. PAYE tax in addition to the agency fees can mean an umbrella company contractor finds himself with far greater overheads and tax liabilities from the off. You are also bound by the terms, conditions and working practices of the umbrella company – which may or may not be restrictive.

Some agencies offer their contractors the option of working through their company – usually referred to as an agency limited company, but the service offered is the same as an umbrella company.

This option is more attractive if your contracts are found to be 'inside' IR35, i.e., you're going to be PAYE taxed at source. Very little point in the overheads of running a limited company if you're already assured of not enjoying any of the benefits.

A summary of the pros and cons:

Good	Bad
Less admin overhead for you	20% less take-home pay
Holiday and sick pay (built up from fees)	Another entity in the pay chain: Client - Agent - Umbrella - You
Familiar tax and national insurance management.	Less flexibility
Quick and easy setup	No control

The main advantages of contracting are the increase in income and the flexibility of being self-employed. And both of these largely disappear with the umbrella option.

That said, the ease of the set up can make it attractive and even sensible for the short term. Provided you are content to pay a 20% premium for the service, contracting is certainly simpler under an umbrella company. There is no need to set up a company, get a bank account, an accountant, register for VAT or basically do anything beyond setting yourself up with the umbrella company, and away you go.

Sole Trader / Partnerships

On the face of it, operating as a sole trader can appear attractive. The company can be set up almost instantly without any of the difficulties associated with setting up a limited company. However, there are three reasons a sole trader arrangement is less desirable to the contractor than either an umbrella or limited company.

Firstly, as previously mentioned, most clients and many agencies will not deal with sole traders. The Income Tax (Earnings and Pensions) Act, 2003 states that where an individual personally provides, or is under an obligation personally to provide services to an end client via an agency, and that individual is subject to (or to the right of) supervision, direction or control as to the manner in which the services are provided; then the income received by the individual under the contract is to be treated for income tax purposes as employment earnings.

This would make the client or agency responsible for all employer and employee National Insurance Contributions (NICs) as well as Pay As You Earn (PAYE) tax. Which would effectively man they had employed you directly, creating precisely the administrative overhead they have sought to avoid by finding a contractor. It is much easier for the agency to insist that contractors manage their own affairs via a limited company or umbrella.

The second reason sole trading is less desirable than other options is that a sole trader does not enjoy the same limited liability the director of a limited company does. In law, a limited company as a separate entity is responsible for its own debts; hence a director will usually escape unscathed. This is less of a concern if you are working in a field where you will not be incurring any debt or holding stock, such as consultancy. However, it is important regardless of operating model to have adequate insurances, notably liability and professional indemnity (more on that later).

Finally, there are tax advantages to operating a limited company. A sole trader will pay Class 2 National Insurance Contributions (NICs) at the prevailing rate, and then Class 4 NICs and income tax on all profits. A director of a limited company can draw a proportion of his or her income via dividends without NICs. The take-home pay of the director will likely be higher than that of the sole trader.

A summary of the pros and cons:

Good	Bad
Simple to set up	Agencies may not work with you
Simple tax and NIC management	Less tax efficient than a limited company
	Sole traders personally liable for any losses

A sole trader approach is really not suitable for a contractor. The lack of willingness of agencies and indeed clients themselves to work with you for fear of becoming liable for your tax and NICs makes this an unwise choice. Once you factor in the drastic reduction in take-home pay even if you did manage to get it to work for your customers, you'll find the price you've paid for simplicity is far too great to consider seriously.

Limited Company

The reality is that when you make the decision to go contracting you will do so under a limited company; the only question is whether you are a director of that company or not.

The limited company route is the most popular one for contractors in the UK for a good reason; it is the structure most familiar to those engaging contractors, and provides maximum return. Setting up and running your own limited company is straightforward once you understand the basics, which will be covered in the next chapter. Once set up it can take as little as 30 minutes a month to run a limited company.

The limited company approach really delivers the advantages of contracting; maximising take home pay, giving flexibility and control as well as safeguarding your personal assets. Limited companies are required by law to file accounts annually but don't let that phase you, you'll have an accountant to support you. A good accountant will let you generate the money while he manages all the paperwork, and that's exactly what you want – to be dedicating your time to billable work. Engaging experts is exactly the right thing to do.

It is important to note that as the director of a limited company, you are not self-employed. You are a company director and consultant employed by your company. The separation between you and your company is absolute, more on that later.

Contracting via your own limited company is absolutely the best bet if you are a business providing services to business (also known as a 'B2B'). This would be consistent with operating outside IR35. If your contract is deemed 'inside IT235' and subject to PAYE tax at source, there is little point in operating your own company, and incurring the related costs, unless other business is also being done, or you see 'inside IR35' as a temporary set of circumstances.

A summary of the pros and cons when outside IR35:

Good	Bad
Higher take home pay, utilising dividends	Some administrative overhead
Expenses can be claimed against anything that is wholly a business cost.	You'll need an accountant (but having one is a good thing!)
Limited liability – personal assets are secure	No sickness or holiday pay, unless you arrange it
Complete control of your Business	Annual filing of accounts
Limited companies have greater credibility in the business world.	Costly if contracting short term, or for very modest sums (sub £25,000)
Accountants' fees are likely to be lower than those of an umbrella.	

It is important to note that the director must take adequate measures to ensure that the contract and working practices agreed with the end client place the work 'outside' IR35 before electing to process pay in any way other than PAYE. More on IR35 later.

Setting up a Limited Company

So, you've decided to set up your own limited company? There are many books dedicated to this subject alone, and there is a tremendous amount of depth and complexity if you want it. But fear not, the kind of bare minimum setup of a limited company you will require to operate as a contractor is actually very simple.

Registering with Companies House

Step one is registering your company with Companies House – which can be completed online in a matter of minutes.

You are required to provide a company name. This name cannot contain words considered sensitive and must be unique. Feel free to be as creative as you like; you can check the availability of a company name with the 'WebCHeck' function on the UK Companies House website. You may also wish to consider availability of Internet domain names, assuming you wish to create a company website, which I recommend you do (though not necessarily on day 1), as well as other branding opportunities, notably in the field of social media. Your company will also need an address for registration. This must be a physical location, and for contractors the popular choices are your home address or your accountant's office address. Unless you're going for the big-time and have rented an office!

Next you will be required to specify officer details. You will need at least one director, who must be over 16. Appointing a company secretary has been optional since 2008, but you can do so should you wish. Each officer will have to provide full name and address details as well as 'consent to act', which consists of confirmation of three pieces of personal information from a selection of seven: town of birth, last 3 digits of telephone number, last 3 digits of National Insurance number, last 3 digits of passport number, mother's maiden name, eye colour and father's first name in lieu of a signature.

The next stage is to confirm shareholder details, as well as the number and class of the shares. It is common for contractors to allocate 100 shares on a percentage basis to all directors, even if all 100 are allocated to the managing director. An accountant can offer advice and any initial decisions made can be changed, although changes attract an administrative fee. Prescribed particulars of rights attached to shares will also need to be supplied (i.e., details of voting, distribution, dividend and any redemption rights attached to the shares). Subscriber authentication information is required and takes the same form as the 'consent to act' requirement above – three of the same seven pieces of information. The declaration now includes details of anyone with a controlling interest in a company, to guard against fraud and tax evasion. If you're setting up a company as a sole director this is very easy, add more details as necessary.

Finally, a payment is required to complete the company registration. It was £15 when this book went to print but modest increases have happened over the years. And that's it! You're now a company director. There are, however, a few more steps required to make your company ready for use as a contractor.

Opening a Company Bank Account

You're going contracting to make money, and you're going to need a bank account for clients and agents to make payments to you. Your company is a separate legal entity and requires a business bank account. Company money is not *your* money, even if you are the sole director of the company. Remember that. I have known a number of people to come unstuck by running the business account like their personal current account. Spend all the money then get a demand for a VAT payment? Awkward.

Most if not all of the high street banks will be very happy to open a business account for you, and you can typically apply online to save yourself time in branch. You will as ever require some basic pieces of information to get started:

Business details

- Contact details
- Business name and address
- Nature of business and legal status
- Start date (if applicable)
- Anticipated turnover
- Funding requirements
- Incorporation details (if Ltd)

Personal details (for both Partners/Directors)

- Personal name and address
- Date you moved into your home address
- Previous address details (if applicable)
- Existing bank account details

As well as date, country and city of birth; and country of nationality and residence.

And with that, a company bank account is created. If you are intending to run a standard consultancy you will likely have no need to borrow money, only to have a bank process payments and keep an account for you. On that basis, the only difference between banks is their fees.

Most banks offer a period of free business banking, usually 18 months. After that introductory period, the typical monthly fees will be a handful of pounds, which will be deducted from the account automatically; the fees are an expense which can be offset against tax. Additional charges are often levied for cheque processing, but most transactions are electronic, so often this isn't an issue. Should anyone pay by cheque, ask them to pay direct in future to save yourself the expense as well as the trouble of physically paying it in.

It is prudent to set up a business bank account with a different bank to that which holds your personal accounts. The Financial Services Compensation Scheme only guarantees funds held by banks to a certain threshold in the event of failure. By spreading your money between institutions, you can safeguard your assets in an uncertain world. You will be allocated a business bank manager when you open the account, who will be interested in talking to you to find out what you need from the bank and what your business aspirations are. For the contractor, this is simple: a receptacle to hold money.

Business bank accounts do not usually pay interest, which is helpful from a simplicity point of view since tax is payable on any interest accrued.

VAT Registration

Registering for Value Added Tax (VAT) is mandatory once company annual turnover reaches a certain threshold – in 2020/21 that threshold is £85,000. Failure to register within 30 days of reaching that threshold can result in a financial penalty for 'failure to notify'.

Although it is not compulsory to register until you actually reach that amount, if you consider it likely that you will exceed the threshold it is simpler to register for VAT from the outset. Doing so has several advantages:

- If you don't keep a close eye on your turnover you may not notice when it passes the threshold. Registering for VAT

early prevents worrying about it later.
- Most people are either aware of the VAT threshold, or associate VAT registration with a 'proper' business. Being VAT registered adds credibility to a fledgling company.
- A key advantage of being VAT registered is the ability to claim back the VAT you have paid on business expenses.
- VAT registration allows you to reclaim VAT from the last four years, provided you have kept proper records and invoices for goods, the time limit for reclaiming VAT on payments for services is six months.
- VAT registration means you'll get a VAT registration number for your business. You must display it on your business stationery and correspondence. Registering from the outset means all your company stationery can be designed from the off without a need to revisit.
- Registering for VAT once trading makes it likely you will have to manage a transition to VAT, invoicing customers for the increased amount and dealing with pro-forma invoices since you are registered from the point you complete the paperwork, but are not given a registration number immediately. Customers cannot reclaim VAT without that registration number.

It is much, much easier to register for VAT immediately if you're fairly sure you'll be troubling the threshold.

Flat rate VAT registration is available up to turnover of £150,000. The concept is simple – the limited company charges VAT on all invoices at the prevailing rate, and then pays the percentage associated with their business activity to HMRC. In the case of consultancy that is currently 16% of the gross invoice figure. There will typically be a modest saving to the company associated with the flat rate scheme, and every little helps!

The only downside to this arrangement is the inability to reclaim VAT on purchases; so the decision to opt for a flat rate VAT registration is an individual one. It is highly likely to make sense for most contractors not incurring significant VATable expenses.

Filing a VAT Return

The downside of VAT registration is the need to file a quarterly return with HMRC. The process is reasonably painless and can be completed online, with the following pieces of information:

- VAT due in this period on sales and other outputs
- VAT due in this period on acquisitions from other EC Member States
- VAT reclaimed in this period on purchases and other inputs (Not Applicable for flat rate VAT registered companies)
- Total value of all sales excluding VAT
- Total value of all purchases excluding VAT
- Total value of all supplies of goods excluding VAT to other EC Member States
- Total value of acquisitions of goods excluding VAT to other EC Member States

You could ask your accountant to submit the return on your behalf, but it is very simple to do yourself. Submission is required 30 days after the end of the 3-month period in question. If, for example, your company's financial year-end is in April, your first quarter would be April to June 30, with a VAT return for that period to be submitted by the end of July (usually you're given until around the 7th of the following month to submit it). Failure to file a return in a timely fashion could again attract a penalty.

In the UK, HMRC have elected to 'Make Tax Digital'. The MTD initiative now demands that all companies above a specific annual turnover file VAT returns electronically, via an approved software product. Many services are available, most cost around £10 a month.

Whilst aggravating that HMRC have seen fit to introduce a fee for something that previously was completely possible manually and without additional cost, the advent of such software does greatly simplify matters. I would probably recommend it, but it is no longer optional regardless, so evaluate products you consider suitable and take your pick. I use Sage, simply because my accountant uses Sage – so I can vouch for the simplicity of their product, as well as its genera usefulness in book-keeping beyond the automation of VAT returns.

Insurance

Some clients and agents may require that consultants have professional indemnity and public liability insurance in place and may also mandate minimum cover requirements for those insurances. Even if the contract you are applying for does not require it, insurance is often a wise investment. The cost is based on your annual turnover, and affordable when set against the losses it protects you against.

Most insurance providers supply packages based on industry sector. Those typical for contractors and consultants follow.

If you are working under an 'inside IR35' contract via an umbrella company, you will typically find the umbrella provides all necessary insurances, saving you the additional cost.

Professional Indemnity

Professional indemnity insurance should be a consultant's main consideration. It provides cover against any claims from a client or agent that you have failed in your duty of care by giving bad advice or making a mistake in your work. It also provides cover against any infringement of intellectual property rights. Many providers will also provide specific cover for loss, theft or damage of client documents in your care, including data – of great value to a contractor.

Public Liability Insurance

Public liability insurance is often associated with business premises, but even if you don't have visitors to your office or home, you could still suffer a public liability claim against your business; for example, if you accidentally damage a client's property in their office. Your staff could trigger a public liability claim if their actions at work injure a client or member of the public.

Employers' Liability Insurance

If you have employees, employers' liability insurance is a legal requirement and is frequently offered as a package with public liability insurance.

The 2004 amendment to the 1969 Employers' Liability (Compulsory Insurance) Act allows only for a company with a single employee to be exempt from the requirement for employers' liability insurance. In practice that means the majority of contractors will be exempt.

However, as a director, you are a company employee, and may feel the insurance to protect employees is a wise investment.

IR35 Insurance

With IR35 legislation consistently on the move in the UK, it is worth considering IR35 insurance. Any such insurance will offer an assessment of a contract to determine status – valuable to the contractor in so far as it removes from him the responsibility of judgement. Assuming a contract has been determined to be 'outside' IR35, the insurance would cover the costs associated with any subsequent investigation, as well as any penalties should they be levied against the contractor and his company.

Such insurance is typically arranged based on the penalty amount required, so spend some time calculating the potential cost of a successful IR35 claim, and progress accordingly.

Potentially worthwhile for peace of mind.

Running a Limited Company

So, everything you needed to know to get going as a contractor has been covered in the previous sections, the most difficult elements are behind you – and it wasn't as difficult as people may have had you believe.

Now that you're up and running you will hopefully be in a contract. Your limited company will need little attention as time passes, and you will likely find five minutes per week more palatable than thirty minutes per month, which again is preferable to one six-hour session a year!

You will need to issue invoices and record expenses, as well as prepare for VAT returns and annual accounts. This will call for some basic book-keeping, but don't be alarmed – I'm a big believer in keeping things simple and with the application of a little technology we can get a personal computer to do most of the hard work.

As Benjamin Franklin famously said - **'An ounce of prevention is worth a pound of cure'.** Setting up a good set of company document templates at the outset will serve you well, and you can find some that have worked handsomely for me on the resources site:

https://www.blackchili.co.uk/bcbooks

Security

We have established in the 'Isn't Contracting Risky?' section that no... it isn't particularly. Well, no more so than having a job in general. There are, however, steps you can take to improve your resilience to unforeseen events.

For instance, what if the client you are working a contract for has a sudden change in budget and serves you your notice? You might only have a week of contract income coming at that point, with a need to hit the contract ads and start talking to agencies as soon as possible. With proper planning, this need not be nerve-racking. Better to build your own security than rely on the goodwill of somebody else to provide it. A key component of the contractor's coping strategy is the reserve fund: money you build over time to carry you through these difficult periods. You should start building it straight away.

A typical contract will have at least a three-month duration, and is likely to pay three to four times an average salary for a similar permanent job. There is a temptation to start enjoying the fruits of your contracting labour, and to splurge a bit with your new income – but I urge you to avoid doing so. If you can continue with the levels of personal and household expenditure you had before you went contracting at least in the short term, you have the opportunity to amass significant reserves in a very short period of time. My recommendation to you is that you aim to hold an amount of money equivalent to **six months' worth of personal and household expenditure**. If you were out of work for six months having not intended to be, there is likely a problem with the market or with you – in terms of skillset versus the contracts you are applying for. In those circumstances the net should be widened to include permanent roles as necessary, or potentially roles outside those you might, in normal circumstances, consider ideal. If you follow the advice in the rest of this book you should, however, never arrive at that point.

Let's use a monthly permanent 'take home' salary of £2000 per month for easy maths, as might perhaps be earned by a project manager. A contract project manager could reasonably expect to achieve £2000 per week and again for easy maths; let's say that equates to £6000 per month available after taxes and other liabilities. An assumption here is that the £2000 permanent salary is roughly equivalent to monthly expenditure. Using the figures above as an example:

- The contractor should hold £12,000 as a reserve fund to cover six months living costs should the need arise.
- At a contract rate equating to £6000 per month, £4000 will be accumulated every month once living costs have been met.
- Holding £4000 per month in reserve for the three-month duration of the contract will result in a £12,000 reserve by the end of the contract.

In following the advice above, the contractor would have amassed a reserve adequate to cover at least six months of living expenses in three months. I have personally never seen a contractor terminated within the initial three months, with 'not renewed' being as bad as it tends to get. Barring any really appalling behaviour or somehow being offered a contract you are in no way qualified to execute.

Once you have amassed a six-month living expense reserve fund; you can start to enjoy your increased income a little with the confidence of knowing you have protected yourself and your household against any unforeseen change in circumstances. For a real-world example of this, after three years of contracting, I started paying myself a year in arrears. This means that I always have at least a year's living expenses in reserve. This gives me the confidence to work as I see fit or to take time off when necessary or desirable. Great for peace of mind and if a contract ends, a contract ends.

You can't put a price on that. You would have to have an incredible permanent job to put yourself in a position to not worry about work for months at a stretch, particularly in a matter of months!

Get a Good Accountant

Running a limited company need not be difficult or time consuming, but I'd like to start this section with a personal recommendation based on my experience. Get a good accountant. It will be the best investment you ever make.

A good accountant possesses the skills and experience to take care of all the financial elements – filing your returns, processing your PAYE and NICs, your payroll, even your VAT should you wish. When I first met my accountant, he said, **'You worry about making the money, and let me worry about everything else'**, and over fifteen years later he has been good to his word. Hopefully, your accountant will be similarly capable.

This book seeks to give an overview of how contractors go about running a business, and how the business of running a business can be simplified. But this book is no substitute for the experience and knowledge of a good accountant. No book is… for that matter.

Get a good accountant. He will save you more than he charges you for his services, and you will not regret it. As an indication, my accountant charges me less than 1% of my annual profits – far less than either an umbrella company administration fee or the amount he saves me every year. There are accountants who will charge less, as well as those who will charge more. Just make sure yours is a good one, and everything else is easy.

When you get to a certain point in earnings, it is also worthwhile seeking professional advice for pensions and investments. Specialists in these areas will, much like a good accountant, charge you significantly less than you will end up saving as a result of following the advice they provide.

Company Website

Establishing a company website is a wise thing to do; you may recall the suggestion in the section dedicated to registering a limited company that you consider availability of domain names when choosing a company name.

These days almost all companies have an internet presence and in exactly the same way as you would research a company or product before making a purchase, potential clients will appreciate being able to get a feel for your company and the service you offer in advance of any engagement.

Creating a website helps build a company and contractor brand, and your website should be publicised via social media, as well as on company stationery, email signatures and so on.

Your website need not be complicated – it can amount to your CV content and preferred contact details. Do remember though that this is a company website, so re-format your CV so it reads as clients your company has provided services to and the services provided. It is very important that a company website represents your company rather than just the contractor as an individual. Setting up a company website is simple, and the process is laid out in this section.

Should you prefer a really easy option, head to **www.web-builder.co.uk** and sign up!

You could have a website up and running using drag and drop style tools in a matter of minutes.

Register a Domain Name

Register a domain name that reflects your limited company name. The .com suffix gives a global feel, where .co.uk distinguishes your company as one located in the United Kingdom. If you have established a limited company, you can use the .ltd suffix but sticking to the suffixes most familiar to Internet users is recommended.

The Internet is a crowded place, and you may find the domain you want is unavailable – some modest invention around the core of the company name should produce a positive outcome. Many people elect to review the availability of suitable Internet domains, as well as usernames on popular social media channels, before selecting their company name.

Another personal recommendation – avoid 'clever' spellings of words in your business name. It gets really old really fast having to spell email addresses for people!

There are an enormous number of companies that will register a domain for you, it will typically cost £10 for two years for a .co.uk domain, and double that for a .com. Be wary of companies that appear to offer low registration fees but tie you in to hosting deals, website design services or even advertising.

You will need to provide your details as domain owner – name, address and contact number, though it is possible to pay a premium not to have these details available to the public. Once you have chosen your domain name, provided your details and paid your money, the domain is yours for the specified time period.

Hosting

Just as a computer needs a disk to store files, your website needs a computer system to reside on. In the world of the Internet this is referred to as hosting, and there are again any number of providers a search box away.

Prices vary significantly but be aware that some of the cheaper offerings may display adverts, limit bandwidth and hence the ability of people to visit your site as well as functionality such as email. Make sure when choosing a hosting provider that you know what you are paying for, and that the service will work for you.

Once you have selected a hosting company you will need to transfer your domain to them, a process that the hosting company will manage on your behalf. Once complete any request for your website will be serviced by the hosting company systems.

The Site

As previously stated, the site need not be complicated. A basic contractor site would include:

- A professional logo – which you can then use on all company stationary.
- A summary of services offered by the company, drawing on your CV for skills, experience and qualifications but

always being mindful that this is a company website.
- Contact details – telephone, mobile, email etc.
- Links to social media presences.

Making the site visually simple can pay dividends. It keeps everything professional and makes maintenance less of an overhead since the site will not look dated in five years. Keeping it simple also means that the design and build of the site can be done by somebody with little to no experience of website design.

Completing the site yourself will save you money, and using web site editing software you would only need to be able to type and embed a logo image to achieve a simple website. Of course, there are numerous web design consultancies who will willingly build a web site for you if you prefer. A simple site will not be expensive and is a worthwhile investment.

It is also possible to download templates for websites which you can customise to your liking, or even to use tools provided by Internet companies to build an entire website from your computer browser with no additional software whatsoever.

Email

Email makes an appearance in this section because typically a hosting company will offer you a specified number of email addresses as part of a hosting package.

The email address you@yourcompany.co.uk helps you look professional in all your dealings with clients, agents and other companies. It also provides the opportunity to separate your work email from personal email, making one or other easy to turn off, ignore or filter as the need arises.

Bookkeeping

As mentioned, running a limited company means dealing with a small amount of paperwork. Some simple bookkeeping skills will be an advantage, but do not despair if you don't have any bookkeeping experience, a bit of common sense and a calculator will get you to where you need to be.

Examples of all the types of documents you will need can be found on the resources site:

https://www.blackchili.co.uk/bcbooks

Since the 'Making Tax Digital' initiative mandated approved software to file VAT returns, and assuming you have purchased such software, you will likely use this for bookkeeping. This is a fantastic improvement to workflow, ensuring accuracy and enabling easier tracking of your business affairs. It is not a substitute for your own records though – I have found myself that Internet-based services frequently become unavailable, and paper records are always helpful regardless.

Your accountant would no doubt be very happy to do all the book-keeping for you, but you can save yourself money by doing it yourself, as well as making sure you have an intimate awareness of your financial position at all times.

Documents that are worth keeping follow.

Invoice Summary

An invoice summary document will help you on an on-going basis, as well as be invaluable to you and your accountant when the financial year-end arrives.

It is recommended that you keep quarterly summary sheets to coincide with your VAT return periods.

The invoice summary should include the following:

Invoice number
Client being invoiced
Total amount invoiced
Date of invoice
Expenses (split by category)
VAT

An example is shown on the following page, and a template can be downloaded from the resource site:

https://www.blackchili.co.uk/bcbooks

<<INSERT COMPANY LOGO HERE>>

Invoice Summary 2015 - 2016 Q1

Invoice Number	Customer	Amount	Date Issued	Date Paid	Travel	Accom	Sub	Other	Total Expenses	VAT Return	VAT Claim	NI (10%)	TAX	Remainder
1	Customer 1	£ 1,000.00	01/01/15		£ 10.00	£ 10.00	£ 10.00	£ 10.00	£ 40.00	£ 166.67	£ -	£ 79.33	£ 158.67	£ 555.33
2	Customer 2	£ 1,000.00	01/01/15		£ 10.00	£ 10.00	£ 10.00	£ 10.00	£ 40.00	£ 166.67	£ -	£ 79.33	£ 158.67	£ 555.33
3	Customer 3	£ 1,000.00	01/01/15		£ 10.00	£ 10.00	£ 10.00	£ 10.00	£ 40.00	£ 166.67	£ -	£ 79.33	£ 158.67	£ 555.33
4	Customer 4	£ 1,000.00	01/01/15		£ 10.00	£ 10.00	£ 10.00	£ 10.00	£ 40.00	£ 166.67	£ -	£ 79.33	£ 158.67	£ 555.33
5	Customer 5	£ 1,000.00	01/01/15		£ 10.00	£ 10.00	£ 10.00	£ 10.00	£ 40.00	£ 166.67	£ -	£ 79.33	£ 158.67	£ 555.33
6	Customer 1	£ 1,000.00	01/01/15		£ 10.00	£ 10.00	£ 10.00	£ 10.00	£ 40.00	£ 166.67	£ -	£ 79.33	£ 158.67	£ 555.33
7	Customer 2	£ 1,000.00	01/01/15		£ 10.00	£ 10.00	£ 10.00	£ 10.00	£ 40.00	£ 166.67	£ -	£ 79.33	£ 158.67	£ 555.33
8	Customer 3	£ 1,000.00	01/01/15		£ 10.00	£ 10.00	£ 10.00	£ 10.00	£ 40.00	£ 166.57	£ -	£ 79.33	£ 158.67	£ 555.33
9	Customer 4	£ 1,000.00	01/01/15		£ 10.00	£ 10.00	£ 10.00	£ 10.00	£ 40.00	£ 166.57	£ -	£ 79.33	£ 158.67	£ 555.33
10	Customer 5	£ 1,000.00	01/01/15		£ 10.00	£ 10.00	£ 10.00	£ 10.00	£ 40.00	£ 166.57	£ -	£ 79.33	£ 158.67	£ 555.33
11	Customer 1	£ 1,000.00	01/01/15		£ 10.00	£ 10.00	£ 10.00	£ 10.00	£ 40.00	£ 166.57	£ -	£ 79.33	£ 158.67	£ 555.33
12	Customer 2	£ 1,000.00	01/01/15		£ 10.00	£ 10.00	£ 10.00	£ 10.00	£ 40.00	£ 166.57	£ -	£ 79.33	£ 158.67	£ 555.33
13	Customer 3	£ 1,000.00	01/01/15		£ 10.00	£ 10.00	£ 10.00	£ 10.00	£ 40.00	£ 166.57	£ -	£ 79.33	£ 158.67	£ 555.33
14	Customer 4	£ 1,000.00	01/01/15		£ 10.00	£ 10.00	£ 10.00	£ 10.00	£ 40.00	£ 166.57	£ -	£ 79.33	£ 158.67	£ 555.33
15	Customer 5	£ 1,000.00	01/01/15		£ 10.00	£ 10.00	£ 10.00	£ 10.00	£ 40.00	£ 166.57	£ -	£ 79.33	£ 158.67	£ 555.33
16	Customer 1	£ 1,000.00	01/01/15		£ 10.00	£ 10.00	£ 10.00	£ 10.00	£ 40.00	£ 166.57	£ -	£ 79.33	£ 158.67	£ 555.33
17	Customer 2	£ 1,000.00	01/01/15		£ 10.00	£ 10.00	£ 10.00	£ 10.00	£ 40.00	£ 166.57	£ -	£ 79.33	£ 158.67	£ 555.33
18	Customer 3	£ 1,000.00	01/01/15		£ 10.00	£ 10.00	£ 10.00	£ 10.00	£ 40.00	£ 166.57	£ -	£ 79.33	£ 158.67	£ 555.33
19	Customer 4	£ 1,000.00	01/01/15		£ 10.00	£ 10.00	£ 10.00	£ 10.00	£ 40.00	£ 166.57	£ -	£ 79.33	£ 158.67	£ 555.33
20	Customer 5	£ 1,000.00	01/01/15		£ 10.00	£ 10.00	£ 10.00	£ 10.00	£ 40.00	£ 166.57	£ -	£ 79.33	£ 158.67	£ 555.33
		£ 20,000.00			£ 200.00	£ 200.00	£ 200.00	£ 200.00	£ 800.00	£ 3,333.33	£ -	£ 1,586.67	£ 3,173.33	£ 11,106.67

VAT @ 20%   £ 3,333.33
Invoice ex. VAT   £ 16,666.67
VAT Return @ 14%   £ 2,333.33

Monies Out

PAYE Salary   £ 1,500.00

If you use the Invoice Summary Microsoft Excel file from **https://www.blackchili.co.uk/bc books** you will find that all the calculations are done automatically for you:

- The figures required for VAT returns
- Flat rate VAT calculations (at 14%, amend as required for your industry).
- The quarterly totals for invoice income and expenditure
- National Insurance Contributions at 10% (an indicative figure for planning purposes)
- Tax at 20% (amend as required)
- The remainder of the invoiced amount minus VAT, expenses, Tax and National Insurance at the standard PAYE rates*

The intention of the invoice summary is three-fold:

1. To give you a 'worst case' scenario re: how much of your invoiced amount you can take without fear of not covering outgoings
2. To automate all the main calculations **
3. To provide your accountant with all the headline figures he will require to process your accounts at the end of the financial year

* Depending on how you structure your affairs, it may be possible to improve upon the default percentages for National Insurance and Tax.

Update the default values to reflect your situation.

** Please do check the calculations in the example spreadsheet – your financial affairs are your responsibility, and yours alone.

If accurately updated, you should find this spreadsheet alone will reduce the paperwork overhead of running a limited company to minutes per month.

It will save you headaches for VAT returns every quarter, in the absence of suitable software, as well as answer any questions your accountant may have. You should find that a good accountant will only require an invoice summary spreadsheet, expense details and your company bank statements to prepare your annual returns.

Invoices

This is a document you're going to be very interested in – it is the one that is used to request payment for services. You want to be paid? You'll need to issue invoices. If contracting via an agency, it will be the agency your company invoices for services.

A basic invoice should show the following:

- Company name and address
- Invoice number
- Client being invoiced (name and address)
- Details of service provided
- Total amount invoiced
- VAT (if applicable)
- Date of invoice
- Terms of payment
- Method(s) of payment

Again, a simple document – but very much required. An example is shown on the following page, and a template can be downloaded from the resource site:

https://www.blackchili.co.uk/bcbooks

<<INSERT
COMPANY
LOGO
HERE>>

<<INSERT COMPANY ADDRESS>>
<<INSERT COMPANY ADDRESS>>
<<INSERT COMPANY TELEPHONE NUMBER>>
VAT Reg.No. <<INSERT VAT NUMBER IF APPLICABLE>>

INVOICE

DATE: 01/01/15
INVOICE #: 1

Bill To:
<<CLIENT NAME>>
<<CLIENT ADDRESS>>
<<CLIENT ADDRESS>>
<<CLIENT ADDRESS>>
<<CLIENT ADDRESS>>
<<CLIENT ADDRESS>>

Ship To:
As billing address

SALESPERSON	P.O. NUMBER	SHIP DATE	SHIP VIA		TERMS
<<INITIALS>>	N/A	As invoice date	N/A		28 days

QUANTITY	DESCRIPTION	UNIT PRICE	AMOUNT
20	Standard Consultancy Days	£500.00	£10,000.00
		SUBTOTAL	£10,000.00
		VAT Rate	20.00%
		VAT total	£2,000.00
		TOTAL	£12,000.00

<<INSERT COMPANY NAME>> BACS Details: <<BANK NAME>> <<SORT CODE>> <<ACCOUNT NUMBER>>
website - <<INSERT WEB SITE ADDRESS>> - email - <<your.name@yourdomain.co.uk>>
company no.<<INSERT COMPANY NUMBER>> | managing director <<INSERT YOUR NAME>>

If you use the invoice template from **https://www.blackchili.co.uk/bcbooks** you will find all the calculations are done automatically for you:

- Quantity multiplied by unit price for a total
- VAT applied at 20% (rate can be changed)
- Total including VAT

Expenses

It is important to keep track of any expenses incurred wholly as a consequence of business activities. You can claim expenses back against tax, lowering your tax bill as well as claiming back VAT depending on your registration status. Commonly, a contractor would consider claiming:

A-Z of typical Contractor expenses – indicative, not exhaustive.

- Accountant's fees
- Air travel
- Bank admin fees
- Computer consumables – must be for business use
- Computer hardware – must be for business use
- Computer software – must be for business use
- Eye tests (where your contracts typically include working at a computer screen)
- Ferries
- Hotel stays (cost must be 'reasonable')
- If you work from home, home office allowance
- Internet connection*
- Meals (when a component of travel expenses)
- Membership of professional organisations
- Mileage – bicycle, can be claimed at 20p per mile
- Mileage – car, at 45p for the first 10,000

and 25p thereafter; keeping fuel receipts is also advised
- Mileage – Motorcycle, can be claimed at 24p per mile
- Mobile phone *
- Parking
- Road tolls
- Stationery
- Subscriptions to trade periodicals
- Taxi fares
- Telephone calls
- Train tickets
- Training

* Company dedicated for a full claim or claim for business use.

Expenses can only be claimed for travel to a temporary place of work. If you have been in the same location for two years, travel expenses may no longer be claimed. This rule has no relationship with the IR35 legislation. Review HMRC's guidance on any change in location. Their focus is on 'material change' to working location to refresh the two-year rule.

Before claiming an expense, satisfy yourself that it passes the 'wholly, exclusively and necessarily for business purposes' test. Always keep receipts – your accountant may not require them, but HMRC will want to see them should they decide your affairs merit scrutiny. Also remember that you are liable for your expense claims and for any underpaid tax that could result, not your company, your accountant or anyone else you take advice from. You should, therefore, be very wary of umbrella companies offering to process expense claims without receipts. The buck stops with you!

The expenses template best suited to you will capture all expenses, likely on a monthly basis. It will include the total expenses incurred for the month, as well as a breakdown of how they were incurred.

If you use the Expenses Microsoft Excel file from **https://www.blackchili.co.uk/bcbooks** you will find the following calculations are done automatically for you:

- Total Expenses
- VAT claim calculated at 20% from manual input of VATable expenses (since not all attract VAT).

<<INSERT COMPANY LOGO HERE>>

Month: 01/01/15
client: <<CLIENT NAME>>

Expenses

Item	£	Notes
Travel:		
Taxis		
Trains		NR1 3JG to IP28 9TZ return trips x 17 (102
Mileage	780.30	miles per day @ 40p)
Other	187.00	34 Toll Rd @ £5.50
Accomodation:		
Hotel		
Subsidence:		
Food etc	3.19	McD 01/01
Other:	1.60	Meeting Parking
	30.00	Weekly office Parking
Total Expenses:	£ 1,002.09	
VATable Expenses:	£ 300.00	
VAT Claim:	£ 60.00	

Claiming all expenses incurred wholly as a consequence of business activity can be worth thousands of pounds a year to a contractor. Make sure you keep all receipts to substantiate your claims.

A competent accountant will be able to advise which expenses you should be claiming. It is well worth taking professional advice.

Bank Statements

The need for company bank statements has been mentioned previously but merits a section in its own right.

Paper statements are worthwhile for your records, as well as being required by your accountant when the time comes to complete your annual returns. Internet banking means these can be printed on demand rather than stored year after year.

Be sure to keep them together and keep them safely somewhere accessible. If you are comfortable completing your banking online, you may be largely unaware of your company bank statements until your accountant asks for them at year-end. Failure to locate the statements will result in a delay in completing your accounts as well as very likely a charge from your bank for re-prints.

An aggravation easily avoided by getting into the habit of filing them safely. Some banks provide a facility to print statement freely from an Internet portal, particularly in the drive toward paperless banking.

Storing Documents

It is typical to keep all documents for seven years and it is recommended that once a financial year is completed, all paper records pertaining to that year be kept together in box files.

A good approach is dividing records into months, and each month into incoming (invoices) and outgoing (expenses and receipts). Keep receipts in envelopes by month to make it easier to find a specific receipt if necessary.

Add four quarterly invoice summaries, a copy of all contracts, any correspondence and your bank statements and you have a full year's documentation in one place. Retain the documents for six years, since that is how far back HMRC may require them.

Company Stationery

Having dealt with the documents that you will need to function as a contractor as well as those that make your life easier, we now come to those that speak of professionalism.

You've got a company website bearing your logo, and you've used that logo on your invoices, expenses and summary paperwork. It makes sense to continue the brand and extend to letter layouts and business cards.

Letters

When you need to write a letter, it pays to look professional. With contracting, this is literal – be it a covering letter for an application to a client or agency, a letter to the bank or your accountant or indeed anything else, it is always best to be professional.

It takes minutes to put together a letterhead and footer template in a word processor, and once you have it… it will be there, ready for years to come. Bringing consistent quality to your company communications.

As ever, you will find an example letter layout on the resource site:

https://www.blackchili.co.uk/bcbooks

<<DATE>>

<<ADDRESSEE NAME>> <<COMPANY LOGO>>
<<ADDRESS>>
<<ADDRESS>>
<<ADDRESS>>
<<ADDRESS>>
<<ADDRESS>>

<<COMPANY NAME & ADDRESS>>
<<COMPANY NAME & ADDRESS>>

tel: +44 (0)111 111 1111
fax: +44 (0)222 222 2222
<<COMPANY WEBSITE>>

<<COMPANY NAME>> registered in england number <<COMPANY NUMBER>>
registered office <<COMPANY ADDRESS>>

Printed on recycled paper

Business Cards

Business cards are a worthwhile investment for the contractor. The nature of the business means that you will be meeting a lot of people in your working life, and the ability to quickly and easily share your contact details is invaluable.

There are various Internet-based business card printers, including some who will provide limited quantities of business cards for free. Whilst this may seem attractive, the free cards generally have advertisements printed on the reverse side and are of a low quality – not the right message to be sending a client.

As with everything else in life, anything worth doing is worth doing well. You can get good quality cards printed in days and for a very reasonable cost. Provided your contact details are not likely to change, they will continue to be usable for years to come. Another opportunity to reuse your company logo and branding, as well as sharing your website, email address and other contact information.

Email Signatures

Email is a standard communication mechanism in the modern business world, and as such it is important that your company communications over email are consistent with other mediums such as your company website, business cards and letterheads.

It takes little time to put together a simple email signature and once completed it can be used automatically by most email client software. A good email signature should include your name, position and contact details as well as links to your company website and any professional directory of which you are a member.

A sample email signature complete with a standard disclaimer, including advice for what to do if a message is received in error and antivirus policy is available on the resource site:

https://www.blackchili.co.uk/bcbooks

Tax

Time for the section you've all been looking forward to!

Although contractors set out to work freelance to enjoy the freedoms and opportunities while taking advantage of the financial benefits of running their own companies, there is no getting around the fact that there is a fair bit to think about.

The good news is that the tax elements of contracting are, once setup, completely straight forward. This section provides some insight on how contractors typically conduct their financial affairs; however, professional advice is recommended unless you are an accountant yourself. Regulations change frequently, so please familiarise yourself with the current position and discuss what is best for your circumstances with your accountant.

The concepts of this section remain valid, but the figures are taken from the 2020/2021 tax year and are subject to change, potentially faster than the content can be revised – so use this section as an introduction, and seek professional advice.

Also keep in mind that, if working inside IR35, many of these taxation elements are not in your control, your umbrella provider will deal with them all on your behalf and pay you a PAYE salary with all deductions already made.

VAT

Value Added Tax is levied on most goods and services provided by registered businesses in the UK. The standard VAT rate is 20%. If your company is VAT registered, you are required by law to add VAT to all your invoices and to collect it on behalf of the UK Government.

Your company pays the VAT collected to HMRC on a quarterly basis. On a £1000 invoice £200 of VAT would be charged, making the invoice total £1200. This helps the turnover figure look healthy, but don't think of the money as yours – it isn't. That knowledge also makes it easier to say goodbye to it at your next quarterly return.

Corporation Tax

As of the 2015 tax year, corporation tax rates have been standardised. They currently sit at 19% but do fluctuate – always around 20% in the UK. Previously, companies with profits over £300,000 per annum were subject to a larger percentage, and those enjoying profits over £1.5m per annum were subject to an even higher corporation tax percentage.

Most contractors would have previously found themselves in the lower bracket based on earnings anyway, but now there is no doubt. Corporation tax is currently 19% of your profits – your invoice totals less VAT and expenses including your PAYE salary.

The deadline for paying any corporation tax owed by your limited company is 9 months after the end of the accounting period. For example, 31 January 2022 for the tax year ending 5 April 2021.

PAYE

Typically, contractors will look to maximise their tax efficiency by receiving a comparatively small salary before drawing the rest of their income as a dividend at a lower tax rate. Such an approach presupposes the contract is deemed 'outside' IR35, since any judged 'inside' are subject to PAYE taxation in their entirety.

All employers are responsible for calculating and collecting taxes owed on their employees' earnings, and the limited company of a contractor is no different.

Every time an employee is paid, the employer sends details of each payment to HMRC. Any taxes owed by the employees are kept aside by the employer, and then subsequently paid to HMRC before the deadline. In practice that means a standing order, of an amount appropriate to cover tax and national insurance, from your company bank account to HMRC monthly to coincide with your PAYE pay.

Your company is then responsible for paying any taxes you owe on your salary to HMRC quarterly.

At the end of each tax year (which runs from 6 April – 5 April), each employee must be given a P60 that details their total earnings (salary) over the previous tax year, minus any deductions.

I have successfully run my own PAYE, but given the amount of time and effort expended in doing so... I can tell you first-hand that this is another area where an accountant is worthwhile. You will not be charged exorbitantly for this service and I wholeheartedly recommend that you instruct your accountant to process payroll on your behalf.

Umbrella company contractors working inside IR35 receive payslips for each working period, and no further action is necessary. The umbrella company will take care of all payroll administration. If you are a company director, your accountant will run a monthly payroll on your behalf as well as updating HMRC in real time, as required by law.

Limited Company Payroll

Should you be interested in saving a few pounds and running your own payroll, the following steps are required:

- Register as an employer with HMRC
- Register every employee on the payroll with HMRC
- Every time you run payroll, update HMRC 'in real time' (RTI)

- Pay any taxes owed by employees to HMRC within the agreed time period

Or to put it another way, let your accountant do it!

Payroll Deadlines

As contractors usually structure their affairs such that their tax liabilities are below the threshold where monthly tax payments become mandatory, quarterly payments of PAYE income tax and NI contributions may be appropriate.

Payments must be made to HMRC within 14 days of the end of the tax month, which falls on the fifth of each month. Payment is, therefore, required on the 19th of the month, or the 22nd if you are making an electronic payment.

Hopefully, you have instructed your accountant to run payroll on your behalf. He will tell you when to pay, and how much. If you are running payroll yourself your accounting software should provide the same service. Once a quarterly standing order for the correct amount has been set up, you need only worry about PAYE and payroll if circumstances change.

Umbrella schemes, of course, take care of all payments as part of their service.

Tax Codes

Every employee has a tax code that tells their employer how much tax is to be deducted from their earnings. The tax code you are assigned is easy to decipher - The initial digits multiplied by 10 indicate the personal tax-free allowance of the individual.

Taxable Benefits

If your company pays for anything that you benefit from personally, such as a company car, you must pay tax on the value of this benefit. All benefits are included on the P11D form. Your tax code may be adjusted to account for these benefits.

Personally, I favour keeping things simple, so if I want a car, I buy a car personally. That approach negates any need to calculate benefit in kind and take it in to account for tax purposes. It also simplifies matters in so far as one never need account for the personal use of an asset, simply claim for the business use of it. In my opinion and experience, that is the easier way to manage such matters.

Again, your accountant will be able to advise you of the approach that best fits your circumstances, but a good rule of thumb to those starting out is to steer clear of potentially taxable benefits and/or seek advice on a case-by-case basis.

Self-Assessment

The PAYE system only deducts tax from wages paid via payroll. Any dividends or other income aside from your PAYE salary will need to be accounted for via the self-assessment system.

If you are a limited company director, you must fill in an annual tax return each year, and if you are an umbrella company employee with untaxed earnings, you are also required to complete a return.

Your accountant may ask you to confirm some additional details, such as any income you receive outside of the limited company, any rental income and details of child benefit receipts. He will then complete the self-assessment on your behalf, requiring only your signature to confirm all the details are accurate.

Companies House Annual Return

As a director of a limited company, you must complete an annual return for Companies House. Companies House will send you an email alert or reminder letter using the details you provided when the company was incorporated.

The due date is usually a year after either:

- The incorporation of your company
- Your last annual return

It is permissible to file your annual returns up to 28 days after the due date, but the penalty for not filing returns by that final cut off is severe – **you can be fined up to £5000 and your company can be struck off**.

Completing an annual return is simple and can again be conducted online via the Companies House Webfiler system. A Companies House annual return includes the following information – and if nothing has changed since your last return, you will simply confirm all information is correct before submitting.

- Company Director and Secretary details
- Company classification
- Type of company
- Registered address
- Address where records are kept
- Statement of capital if shares are allocated
- Details of shareholders

The cost of filing the annual return online is approximately a third of filing by post.

National Insurance

The contractor requires an awareness of Employers' and Employees NICs.

NICs are payable on any salaried income an employee receives. During the 2019/20 tax year, employees must pay NICs of 12% on income between £166 and £962 per week, and at 2% on any income above £962 per week.

If you're working via your own limited company, it is possible to minimise your exposure to NICs by paying yourself a minimal salary. NICs are not payable on company dividends.

All employers must pay NICs on the salaries they pay to their staff. No NICs are payable at all if you draw an annual salary below £8,632, but your accountant will be able to advise you how best to structure your affairs.

Obviously, all these figures are subject to change, so check the prevailing rates and thresholds, and be sure to speak with your accountant.

Umbrella contractors inside IR35 do take a bath here, being responsible for employers as well as employees NI, plus an apprenticeship levy. This can be significant and is part of the reason for the need to increase 'inside' rate to achieve take home parity with 'outside'.

Pensions

Post-IR35, pensions represent one of increasingly few tax breaks available to contractors. Money can be invested directly from the company account saving the income tax that would have been payable as well as both employers and employee's NI contributions. The money then grows tax-free in the pension fund. A pension, therefore, represents a very efficient means to invest, since any alternative option can only be invested in once all tax and NI have been paid. Obviously, it is recommended that the contractor is mindful of his pension arrangements – since leaving permanent employment no one else is going to do it for you!

Pensions of several flavours are available from numerous providers. As a pension is a long-term investment, consideration should be given to the past performance of a provider and fund as indicators of future potential. Also, as the number of new entrants to the market is ever increasing, reliability of provider to still be trading in 20 years is vital. Flexibility is also a key factor in the long term – is the product portable? You may not be contracting forever.

Having read this book, it may not surprise you to hear that I took the most straightforward option, namely to take the personal pension my permanent employer enrolled me in many years ago and continue contributions as an individual. This may not be the best course of action for you, but it is likely an option worth considering given how much work you have to do to get going as a contractor. It can be nice occasionally to just take the easy option.

Perhaps as a contractor you have neglected your pension for a number of years whilst focusing on other priorities or making other investments. Fear not – it is possible to invest significant sums every year in a pension fund with no penalty, so catching up is very achievable. It is also possible to use any unused tax-free contributions allowance of previous years to bolster those of the current year – professional advice can be a very worthwhile investment here.

Personal pensions and stakeholder pensions are broadly similar these days with fees having broadly fallen in line. An executive pension may be an interesting option but be aware that the higher level of contributions available comes at the cost of higher fees from the provider.

If you have a pension, consider continuing. If you don't, or you want to ensure you make the best of your investment in your circumstances, seek professional advice and consider the available options.

IR35

Another section I'm sure you've struggled not to skip straight to! IR35 legislation has gained some notoriety since its inception in 2000 and is famed for complexity. I hope to explain clearly and concisely, albeit in simple terms.

What is it?

IR35 is essentially the HMRC response at the turn of the century to an increasing number of permanent employees leaving their jobs on a Friday, only to return on Monday as freelance consultants.

The contractor consultant was happy with his increase in take-home pay. The client was happy having discharged himself of the responsibilities of an employer. The exchequer was less pleased with the reduction in tax receipts owing to the dramatic reduction in employers National Insurance Contributions, as well as the lower rate of tax on dividends versus PAYE.

IR35 was developed as a means for HMRC to identify 'disguised employees' – those workers supplying their services to clients via an intermediary such as a limited company. Workers operating in such a way that they would be an employee if the intermediary was not used. Enabling recovery of any tax or national insurance owing for a period up to the last six years.

However, if you are a genuine contractor running a legitimate business, you have nothing to fear from IR35. HMRC investing more in IR35 investigations than it ever recouped in tax is well publicised.

However, it is also fair to note that in shifting the responsibility of IR35 determinations to the end client, along with any penalties and other consequences of getting it wrong, IR35 has succeeded in the majority of contractors being deemed 'inside', whether they really are or not.

Inside or Outside?

The common terminology of IR35 categorises contracts as being either inside or outside of IR35. Contracts undertaken as if an employee will be deemed inside IR35, the contract is then subject to PAYE tax and national insurance at the prevailing rates for income resulting from that contract. Or the contract is deemed outside of IR35, and the contractor invoices the client for the full amount, before being free to pay himself via a limited company in whatever manner he sees fit.

Recent developments included a presumption that any contractor working in the public sector would be considered to be 'inside' IR35 by default, with extremely limited potential to argue otherwise. That same logic will be rolled into the private sector, at least to large companies in April 2021 (at the time of writing). The responsibility for determining IR35 status lies with the hiring company, though the contractor can make representations. This development has seen a shift in engagements, from a contract based on duration only - 6 months at £500 a day, to contracts based on specific projects and outcomes. Having contracts assessed for IR35 status is worthwhile, a service available via the insurance discussed previously. You then have two options - take the contract, and be bound by its terms and consequences, or seek another with which you are happier.

There are two main criteria by which a contract's IR35 status will be judged beyond the default, should HMRC decide to take an interest – the contract between your limited company and the agency, and your working practices with the client. Both could be scrutinised fully, and HMRC have the capability to demand all documents as well as being able to contact both agency and client directly whilst making enquiries. There is more weight to working practices than the contract itself.

It is very important to make sure if you are operating outside of IR35, that your contracts and working practices support that status. Previously all responsibility for this lay with the contractor, now the contractor is only responsible for correcting any additional taxes that may be considered payable if subsequent review deems a contract 'inside'.

The Key Criteria

In addition to the creeping default 'inside' judgement, there are three main elements of a written contract and working practice that are scrutinised to establish whether the contractor is operating as an employee, and hence the contract is inside IR35:

- Control – Does the client control the contractor? Location, start time, length of day, the scope of work and how that work should be completed, the presence of a line manager. If the client closely controls the contractor, the contract is inside IR35.
- Substitution – Do you have the right of substitution, and more importantly could you exercise it? Can you send another company employee in your place to complete any required tasks? Do you hire staff or subcontract to others? If a contract has to be executed by you personally you could be seen as an employee, and inside IR35.
- Mutuality of Obligation – There is a mutuality of obligation between client and contractor if the client is obliged to provide paid work and the contractor is obliged to accept it. If a contractor is working on a specific project and the client requests an additional piece of work outside the original contract scope be completed, mutuality of obligation could be implied by the contractor

agreeing to complete that additional work.

Some contracts are designed to be 'IR35 compliant'. They will contain clauses that place control in the hands of the contractor, establish the right of substitution and establish no mutuality of obligation.

However as previously noted, the more important element is that these criteria are in your favour in day-to-day execution under contract.

What if I'm inside IR35?

If your contract is inside IR35, the appropriate course of action is to pay all your invoice income less limited company fees and expenses to yourself as a PAYE salary whilst paying appropriate income tax and NICs. In paying yourself in full as an employee, you are complying with IR35 regulations. If the client you are working for, or their agent, adjudges the contract to be inside IR35 the decision will be taken for you and they will pay you via PAYE – removing the need for you to manage payroll.

If you are operating outside IR35, HMRC can scrutinise your contracts for the last six years, and could deem them inside IR35, resulting in a potentially significant bill for income tax, NICs, penalties and interest. Should you find yourself in this situation you will need to calculate the deemed payment on your income. Deduct PAYE salary, a 5% expenses allowance and pension contributions then take what is left and calculate any tax and NIC liabilities.

After all that negativity, I should also point out that very few people are investigated annually. Expert analysis of contracts and working practices is available, as is comprehensive insurance to provide peace of mind against the initial investigation as well as any eventual penalties. It is also likely that both contracts and working practices will evolve with legislation to enable contractors to operate under the auspices of a company, clients to be able to engage the services of contractors where necessary, and HMRC to recover appropriate taxation from all concerned.

IR35 Compliance

There are several things the contractor can do to minimise exposure to IR35, all of which unsurprisingly focus on two complementary elements – operating as a limited company and not appearing to be an employee of any client.

Obviously, you should see that **contracts** are written in an IR35 compliant manner as well as having the contracts and your working practices reviewed by an expert. There are example contracts for both agency and direct client engagements available on the resource site – no magic IR35-compliance promises, but they're a good start:

https://www.blackchili.co.uk/bcbooks

To establish your limited company service offering and minimise any potential for confusion for an employee you should consider:

- In all your dealings, remember that you are a company providing services to a business.
- Taking previously offered advice to set up a company website and have business cards and other stationery printed.

- Working from home or renting an office.
- Paying for your own training courses.
- Using your own equipment – laptops, stationery, etc.
- Not using a subsidised staff canteen or similar client facility.
- Not participating in client-funded social events
- Exercising your right of substitution.
- Demonstrating control over your working time and practices.
- Taking advantage of tax liability and IR35 insurance.

In so doing, you would demonstrate that you are operating as a company, not an individual. That you are not an employee operating within an artificial employment construct. That you operate with autonomy and are taking risks yourself, rather than sheltering with any employer.

IR35 Enquiries

If HMRC believe your working practices warrant investigation, you will receive a letter requesting a breakdown of your company income for the specified accounting period(s), copies of all contracts associated with that income and any evidence you feel substantiates your opinion that your contracts and working practices are outside IR35.

You have approximately one month to comply with the request. Keep in mind that HMRC can and do contact clients and agencies to validate documents and the evidence you provide.

If you are contacted for an IR35 review, you should contact your IR35 insurance provider immediately. You should also contact your accountant and request assistance in collating the required information. Keep in mind that your accountant is likely to charge you for time expended in the preparation of the required materials as well as any time spent representing you at an HMRC hearing.

IR35 Recommendations

As in all areas of business and particularly when it comes to matters of law and potentially significant financial consequences, it pays to consult the experts if you are not one yourself.

Talk to your accountant; get contracts checked by IR35 specialists. Take all steps you can to ensure there is no prospect of you being confused for an employee in delivering company services. Make sure that your working practices reflect your contract and again that you are conducting yourself as a company providing services to the client.

Provided you are a genuine contractor providing services to clients and not operating as an employee of the client organisation, you have nothing to fear from IR35. Your contract will be reviewed, and the judgement is not yours to make, unless you are suitably qualified and situated.

However, given the complexity of the legislation, the subtleties of interpretation, the ever-changing landscape and the consequences of a review in HMRC's favour set against the modest cost of tax liability and IR35 insurance my parting recommendation has to be to take out appropriate insurance, if you are in any doubt. Doing so will give you access to specialists to review contracts for IR35 compliance from the outset, for the insurer it minimises their exposure to risk, and the contractor gets the peace of mind of knowing it isn't only him who thinks he is operating in line with all applicable regulations.

IR35 status determinations are now made by end-clients, and therefore the only involvement for a contractor is accepting a contract, or not, based on that determination. As before, look for a 30% premium to pull an inside IR35 contract's take-home pay in line with an outside IR35 contract.

If called upon to debate the status of a contract you are already in, make representations you can substantiate around your working practices.

Maximising your Income

If you're working via an umbrella company or on a PAYE basis with any client or agency, income tax and NICs will be deducted at source and paid to HMRC on your behalf. There is, therefore, no maximisation of income available, your wages are fixed by your contract rate, umbrella admin fee and prevailing tax and NIC rates.

It is considered most tax-efficient for a limited company director to receive a salary close to the personal tax-free allowance. The company will receive corporation tax relief at 20% on that salary, and the director will not have any income tax liabilities on that component of earnings. The balance of any company profits after corporation tax can then be paid as a dividend, subject to tax at the prevailing rate.

It is worth considering state benefits. If you receive a salary over the lower earnings limit for National Insurance you are generating NI credits for state benefits such as Jobseeker's Allowance, Incapacity Benefit, State Retirement Pension and Maternity Allowance.

Everybody gets a tax-free income allowance. The basic rate of income tax applies to income over and above the personal tax-free allowance, and up to the figure at which higher rate income tax applies.

This means that a contractor who stays inside the basic rate income tax band any additional personal tax liabilities, since corporation tax has already been deduced from company profits. Any additional income would then be taken in the form of dividends, which again have a tax-free allowance albeit a fairly modest one. Over and above this, dividends are taxed, but at a preferential rate when compared to income tax of the same amount.

Contractors will often seek to employ their spouse in the company. Perhaps appointing them as shareholders of the company to take advantage of dividend allowances. Seeking advice is recommended here, since there are several potential pitfalls, and the best course of action is highly dependent on your circumstances.

A spouse must, however, have a demonstrable role in the company for this approach to pass HMRC rules.

Taking Holiday

One of the joys of contracting is being able to take holiday whenever you like and without restriction. You are operating as a company and hence have whatever holiday entitlement you want to grant yourself.

It is important, however, to keep in mind that the client has the entitlement to stop paying your invoices or cease any contract if you fail to provide the services they require.

With that in mind, I advocate a simple approach. Do not take any holiday during periods of work where billable hours would be lost if it can possibly be avoided. The reasons for this are very simple – you will maximise the income from a contract at the same time as providing the client with the service required. This greatly improves your immediate prospects as well as making a renewal more likely.

When a contract naturally finishes an opportunity for taking a holiday follows. The advantage of taking holiday here is minimising the financial impact by not losing any potentially billable hours. Should you find another contract before your current one has ended, negotiate a start date one week later – your holiday will be all the more relaxing knowing you will be returning to a contract afterwards.

The Contract Market

The contract market has been a consistently good performer for over 20 years. As you will see from a simple search of your favoured job listings Internet site for your current role, your skills are in demand.

You are likely to find dozens of roles that fit your skills, and to see rates up to four times a typical salary for the same position on a permanent basis.

Some flexibility will serve you well. You may find it advantageous to consider a longer commute than you might usually aim for if the contract is particularly promising, interesting or lucrative. If the contract is based some distance from your home and seeking local accommodation becomes attractive, it is likely you will be able in time to negotiate working from home for a proportion of the week, or an early finish on a Friday to travel home in exchange for longer days through the rest of the week.

There are some peaks and troughs in the market that are well established. For example, it can be difficult to secure a contract between late November and mid-January for the simple reason that clients are mindful that Christmas will disrupt any imminent programme of work. Hiring managers may also be on holiday. However, there can be opportunities in the same period to provide cover for any permanent staff members taking holiday, or if the client is planning significant work during the traditionally quiet seasonal period.

Similarly, it can take longer to secure a contract in the summer months, owing to key personnel being on annual leave.

Many companies structure their year-end to coincide with the financial year-end in April. Consequently, you will often find client budgets are being stretched from March into April. Rates may be lower and securing a contract harder. Immediately after the change in financial year by mid-April, clients will have their New Year budget available. Rates will improve and contracts will be easier to secure.

There are no hard and fast rules, but there are definite cycles to the contract market. Being aware of some of the background trends as well as mindful of any industry specific ebbs and flows will make it easier for the contractor to position himself optimally, maximising his rate and securing his next contract.

Training

Once you make the transition to contracting training becomes more accessible, albeit self-funded. It is more important than ever to keep your skills up to date and investing in annual training is worthwhile when it comes to maximising rates and saleability.

Training can be costly, consider:

- The true cost of training, including any lost billable hours
- Any associated expenses – accommodation, exam fees, food, travel
- Can you reclaim the VAT?

Condensed residential courses can appear a more costly option at first glance, but once you consider the shorter timescales mean fewer lost billable hours, they become more attractive. Talk to the training company and explain you are self-funding, often they may consider reducing the price if you sound as if you're ready to sign up. Likewise, take advantage of the flexibility of contracting by booking as close as possible to the course commencement date. Training providers will likely have class space they want to fill to maximise their income. There are bargains to be found.

The Contractor Talent Matrix lists skills, qualifications and experience as key weapons in the arsenal of the modern contractor. Training represents value as it offers opportunity to improve both skills and qualifications in a single act.

On-going training and development is vital to the successful contractor in a competitive marketplace. Research your market well and establish what skills and qualifications are in demand or considered a standard for the contracts you want to secure. Then go and earn those qualifications.

Typically, a residential training course lasting a week will cost approximately the same as a typical contractor invoices his customer for a week. An investment that will in my experience pay for itself within a year. Your rate will increase, you may be able to reach up to the next rung in seniority terms, and you'll spend less time looking for work. And all that in addition to broadening your skill base. It's a win from every angle!

IR35 Developments

What began as a set of guiding principles designed to detect 'disguised employment', soon became a presumption that any contractor working in the public sector would be 'inside' IR35 by default, with limited opportunity to argue otherwise. That same logic will soon be rolled into the private sector, at least to large companies. We could be looking at the end of contracting!

That doesn't seem likely – legislation is likely to be reviewed, and change is all but certain. Nevertheless, it is likely that a vast majority of contractors will find themselves 'inside' IR35. The responsibility for determining IR35 status lies with the hiring company, and being risk averse, those companies are very likely to play it safe and declare contracts inside IR35. Probably as a default, in spite of the direction not to make blanket judgements. Options in this scenario are limited:

- Argue contract status. You're not likely to win.
- Negotiate a rate increase to at least partially offset any increase in tax liabilities.
- Consider working as a freelancer consultant – many agents will offer PAYE settlements, holiday pay and the trappings of employment.
- Consider permanent opportunities.
- Work inside IR35, and if you genuinely believe you are not, make

representations to the tax authorities to recover overpaid taxes.

My main criticism of this legislation, aside from the fact it will recover less tax than contractors are already paying... is that in seeking to correct a perceived imbalance between the employed and self-employed, it makes working circumstances substantially worse for the self-employed. Get taxed like an employee, without any of the benefits? Sounds like a terrible idea to me.

For similar reasons, taking a PAYE quasi-permanent job with an agency seems a terrible idea. They will be paying you less than a client would (having taken a commission out of the amount the client gave them to secure you), they will offer you fewer benefits and no job security.

There are only two realistic options for the contractor – only take outside IR35 contracts, and ensure your working practices reflect that status, or work inside IR35 having negotiated suitable compensation.

Or...

So You've Going Permie?

I didn't think I would ever be writing this section, but times change. If your contract, job type, industry or working practices place you inside IR35, or highly likely to be, you might be considering a return to the world of permanent employment.

Nothing wrong with that. As discussed previously, many contractors will be thinking similarly, reviewing their options and weighing up the pros and cons. Many will be expecting to return to permanent work for a short time to let the dust settle around the contract market, with a view to making a return as soon as the opportunity arises.

Let's get the main 'con' out of the way first – money. It is extremely unlikely a client will offer a contractor an equivalent permanent salary and package to their previous contract rate. There is a partial explanation for this in the form of employers' National Insurance – which could account for a salary offer of approximately 12.5% less than the annualised contract rate by way of salary. Offers to contractors in recent times have indicated a reduction of more like 25% which is, in my opinion, largely opportunistic.

Less scrupulous employers will spot the opportunity to 'low ball' contractors, whom they see as short on time and therefore options, with a view to securing high calibre staff at bargain prices. Do not be rushed or pressured.

Keep in mind that you worst case scenario (assuming your contract role still exists) is being declared inside IR35. There are several calculators available on the end of a simple Internet search which will tell you what your hourly or daily rate equates to as a permanent salary, whether you're inside or outside IR35. Use this information as a foundation for negotiations around permanent employment opportunities – employing you will cost a client more than giving you a contract role, but not necessarily as much as they would have you believe.

Weigh up any offer – what are you getting that is of use to you? Here come the 'pros'.

Salary plus benefit in the form of pension contributions, a car, five weeks holiday, paid sickness and bank holidays, maybe some private health coverage. All very useful, and of interest. Perhaps there is an offer of training, which could be very useful to the long-term contractor whose skills on paper are not as up to date as they could be.

Maybe after being a freewheeling consultant, responsible for his own professional destiny, you would enjoy a sense of being a proper part of a team rather than the overpaid consultant adjacent to it. Perhaps you would like the feeling of security that accompanies paid employment, even if your contractor sensibilities don't quite allow you to believe it.

I would not for an instant suggest permanent employment is without value, or not worth considering, but always remember you have options.

The contract market is not going anywhere, and flexible staff will always be required. It is likely that rates will increase to offset any decline in earnings, and also likely that regulatory environments will improve as changes bite. It is probable that new enablers for contracting within those regulatory frameworks will surface as the new climate is better understood.

The Resource Site

On the resource site for this publication at **https://www.blackchili.co.uk/bcbooks** you will find example documents and templates for the following:

- Agency Contract
- Client Contract
- CV
- Expenses Calculator
- Expenses Recording
- Invoice Summary
- Sample Invoice
- Letter Template
- Email Signature

The system I have developed works well for me and has supported my accountant in processing my annual accounts as well as helping me complete quarterly VAT returns with minimal time and effort for a decade. Even before the advent of mandatory bookkeeping software!

I encourage you to develop your own tools to simplify processes, particularly those you complete regularly.

So You're Going Contracting Too!

So... you're aware of the benefits of contracting as a professional – financial, flexibility and self-employment.

I've introduced the contractor talent matrix and the balance required between skills, qualifications and experience as well as how you can go about addressing any shortfall – increasing your saleability as well as maximising rates. We've walked through the process of securing your first contract and of setting yourself up in business so you can start making some money.

You will have learned that setting up and running a limited company is not complicated, can be achieved in a relatively short period of time and at a modest cost. We have reviewed the basics of the many taxes of which you need to be aware, as well as ways a typical contractor will conduct his affairs to make best use of his resources.

I hope this book has achieved what it set out to – to demystify contracting and let you in on how the professionals do it.

It doesn't have to be difficult and provided you have a solid talent matrix it isn't risky. There are no significant drawbacks to contracting that do not exist in the world of work more generally, and I truly believe that more and more people will be contracting as the years go by and clients demand flexibility. If I'm right, it will pay to be ahead of the curve.

So what are you waiting for? Trust me, if I can do it... so can you.

Contacting the Author

If you have any comments on this book, questions for me or suggestions for the next edition you can contact me at the following address:

publications@blackchili.co.uk.

You will also find my professional profile on LinkedIn here:

https://www.linkedin.com/in/renhimself/

Printed in Great Britain
by Amazon